iPhone FOR DUMMIES

Cheat Sheet

Five Keys to Mastering Multitouch

The iPhone has no physical keyboard or keypad buttons, so you have to use a virtual version of buttons and controls that appear on-screen as required for the tasks at hand. Prep your fingers for the following (see Chapter 2 for details):

- ✔ Flick a finger to scroll through music, pictures, e-mails, contacts, and more.
- ✔ Tap against the screen to open applications, play songs, choose photos, and so on.
- ✔ Pinch and unpinch to enlarge Web pages and pictures, or make them smaller. The actions involve placing your thumb and index finger against the screen. Then keeping the thumb in place, drag your index finger to pinch or unpinch accordingly.
- ✔ Trust the virtual keyboard. It makes suggestions and corrects mistakes on-the-fly.
- ✔ Correct errors by holding your finger against the screen to bring up a magnifying glass that lets you position the pointer in the precise spot that needs to be edited.

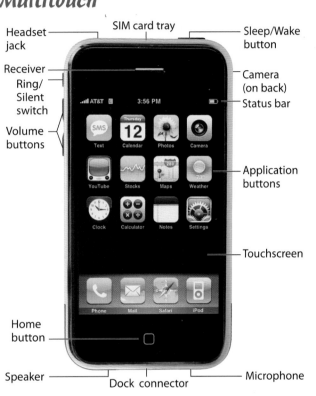

Headset jack
SIM card tray
Sleep/Wake button
Receiver
Ring/Silent switch
Volume buttons
Camera (on back)
Status bar
Application buttons
Touchscreen
Home button
Speaker
Dock connector
Microphone

Five Ways to Make a Phone Call

You have several options for making a phone call after tapping the Phone icon on the Home screen, and then tapping one of these icons, as outlined in Chapter 4:

- ✔ **Contacts:** Scroll through the list of contacts until you find the person you want to call. Tap the person's name and then tap the appropriate phone number (such as home or mobile).
- ✔ **Favorites:** This is the iPhone equivalent of speed dialing, or the list of people (and the specific numbers) you call most often. Tap the listing and iPhone dials.
- ✔ **Recents:** Tapping the Recents icon displays the iPhone call log. Recents houses logs of all the recent calls made or received, as well as calls that you missed. Tap anywhere on a name to return a call.
- ✔ **Keypad:** Manually dial on a virtual touch-tone keypad.
- ✔ **Voicemail:** Through visual voicemail, you can listen to voicemail messages in any order you want, not just in the order in which the messages arrived. To play back a voicemail, tap the name or number in question and then tap the tiny play/pause button that shows up to the left. Returning a call is as simple as tapping the green Call Back button.

For Dummies: Bestselling Book Series for Beginners

Working with Contacts

You access your address book by tapping the Phone icon on the Home screen. (There's no address book icon.) Here are some of the things you can do with contacts in the Phone application:

- ✔ **Create a new contact:** Tap Contacts at the bottom of the screen, and then tap the + button in the upper right. Enter the contact information and then tap Save.

- ✔ **See contact info from the Favorites, Recents, or Voicemail screen:** Tap the right arrow next to the message. The contact's information appears. Tap the contact's phone number or e-mail address to contact the person by phone or e-mail.

- ✔ **Add a caller to your contacts:** Tap Recents or Voicemail and then tap the right arrow next to their number. Tap Create New Contact, enter the contact information, and then tap Save.

- ✔ **Add a contact after dialing a number with the keypad:** Enter the number on the numeric keypad and then tap the icon that's a little + with a person on its right, in the lower-left corner of the screen. Then either tap Create New Contact and enter the contact information or tap Add to Existing Contact and choose a contact. When you're finished, tap Save.

Five Things to Try When Your iPhone Acts Up

Most of the time your iPhone behaves itself, but every so often it doesn't. Chapter 14 delves into this dilemma in much more detail, but this is the cheat sheet, so here's a quick review of things you can try if your iPhone misbehaves.

1. **Restart it.** Press and hold the Sleep/Wake button, and then slide the red slider to turn it off. Wait a few seconds. Press the Sleep/Wake button to turn it back on.

2. **Force any frozen applications to quit.** Press and hold the Home button on the front of the iPhone for 6 to 10 seconds. Then restart it (see Step 1).

3. **Reset it.** Press and hold the Sleep/Wake button while you press and hold the Home button at the same time. This forces your iPhone to restart.

4. **Reset iPhone settings.** Tap the Settings icon on your Home screen, and then tap General, Reset, and Reset All Settings. Resetting iPhone settings won't erase your data, but you'll probably have to change some settings afterwards.

5. **Restore it.** Connect your iPhone to your computer as though you were about to sync. Then select the iPhone in the iTunes source list and click the Restore button on the Summary tab.

Be aware that clicking the Restore button will erase all the data and media on your iPhone and reset all its settings.

Because your data and media (except photos you've taken and contacts, calendar events, and On-the-Go playlists you've created or modified since your last sync) still exist on your computer, you shouldn't lose anything. Your next sync will take longer, and you will have to reset any settings you've changed since you got your iPhone. But your media and data files shouldn't be affected.

For Dummies: Bestselling Book Series for Beginners

iPhone™

FOR

DUMMIES®

iPhone™
FOR
DUMMIES®

by **Edward C. Baig**
USA TODAY Personal Tech columnist

and
Bob LeVitus
Houston Chronicle "Dr. Mac" columnist

BICENTENNIAL
1807
WILEY
2007
BICENTENNIAL

Wiley Publishing, Inc.

iPhone™ For Dummies®

Published by
Wiley Publishing, Inc.
111 River Street
Hoboken, NJ 07030-5774

www.wiley.com

Copyright © 2007 by Wiley Publishing, Inc., Indianapolis, Indiana

Published by Wiley Publishing, Inc., Indianapolis, Indiana

Published simultaneously in Canada

For general information on our other products and services, please contact our Customer Care Department within the U.S. at 800-762-2974, outside the U.S. at 317-572-3993, or fax 317-572-4002.

For technical support, please visit www.wiley.com/techsupport.

Wiley also publishes its books in a variety of electronic formats. Some content that appears in print may not be available in electronic books.

Library of Congress Control Number is available from the publisher.

ISBN: 978-0-470-17469-2

Manufactured in the United States of America

10 9 8 7 6 5 4 3 2

About the Authors

Edward C. Baig writes the weekly Personal Technology column in *USA TODAY* and is co-host of the weekly *USA TODAY*'s Talking Tech podcast. He is also the author of *Macs For Dummies*, 9th Edition, for Wiley Publishing. Before joining *USA TODAY* as a columnist in 1999, Ed spent six years at *Business Week,* where he wrote and edited stories about consumer tech, personal finance, collectibles, and travel, among other topics. He received the Medill School of Journalism 1999 Financial Writers and Editors Award for contributions to the "*Business Week* Investor Guide to Online Investing." That followed a three-year stint at *U.S. News & World Report*, where Ed was the lead tech writer for the News You Can Use section but also dabbled in other subjects. He recalls fondly putting together features on baseball card investing, karaoke machines, and the odd things people collect, including Pez dispensers, vintage radios, and magic memorabilia.

Ed began his journalist career at *Fortune* magazine, gaining the best basic training imaginable during his early years as a fact checker. Through the dozen years he worked at the magazine, Ed covered leisure-time industries, penned features on the lucrative dating market and the effect of religion on corporate managers, and also started up *Fortune*'s Products to Watch column.

Bob LeVitus, often referred to as "Dr. Mac," has written or co-written 50 popular computer books, including *Dr. Mac: The OS X Files* and *Mac OS X Leopard For Dummies* for Wiley Publishing; *Stupid Mac Tricks* and *Dr. Macintosh* for Addison-Wesley; and *The Little iTunes Book*, 3rd Edition and *The Little iDVD Book*, 2nd Edition for Peachpit Press. His books have sold more than a million copies worldwide. Bob has penned the popular Dr. Mac column for the *Houston Chronicle* for the past ten years and has been published in dozens of computer magazines over the past fifteen years. His achievements have been documented in major media around the world. (Yes, that was Bob juggling a keyboard in *USA Today* a few years back!)

Bob is considered one of the world's leading authorities on Mac OS. From 1989 to 1997, he was a contributing editor and columnist for *MacUser* magazine, writing the Help Folder, Beating the System, Personal Best, and Game Room columns at various times. In his copious spare time, Bob heads up a team of expert technical consultants who do nothing but provide technical help and training to Mac users via telephone, e-mail, and Internet-enabled remote control software, which allows them to see and control your Mac no matter where in the world you may be. If you're having problems with your Mac, you ought to give them a try. You'll find them at www.boblevitus.com or 408-627-7577.

Dedications

I dedicate this book to my beautiful wife, Janie, for making me a better person every day I am with her. And to my incredible kids: my adorable little girl, Sydney (one of her first words was "iPod"), my infant son, Samuel (who is all smiles from the moment he wakes up in the morning), and, of course, my "canine" son, Eddie. I am madly in love with you all.

—Ed Baig

This book is dedicated to my wife, Lisa, who taught me almost everything I know about almost everything except computers. And to my children, Allison and Jacob, who love their Macs almost as much as I love them (my kids, not my Macs).

—Bob LeVitus

Authors' Acknowledgments

Special thanks to everyone at Apple who helped us turn this book around so quickly: Katie Cotton, Natalie Kerris, Greg (Joz) Joswiak, Bob Borchers, Keri Walker, Jennifer Hakes, Jennifer Bowcock, and everyone else. We couldn't have done it without you.

Big-time thanks to the gang at Wiley: Bob "Can't you work any faster?" Woerner, Susan "Patience-is-my-middle-name" Pink, Andy "The Boss" Cummings, Barry "Still no humorous nickname" Pruett, and our technical editor Dennis R. Cohen, who did a rocking job in record time as always. And extra-special thanks to Kevin Kirschner, Clint Lahnen, and Shelley Lea for their patience and persistence in setting up the photo shoots and taking the pictures to make this book look as great as it does. Finally, thanks to everyone at Wiley who we don't know by name. If you helped with this project in any way, you have our everlasting thanks.

Bob adds: Thanks also to super-agent Carole "I won't call you Swifty in my next book" McClendon, for deal-making beyond the call of duty, yet again. You've been my agent for more than twenty years and you're *still* the greatest. And thanks also to my family and friends for putting up with me during this book's gestation. Finally, thanks to Saccone's Pizza, Home Slice Pizza, The Iron Works BBQ, Chuy's, Diet Coke Zero, and ShortStop for sustenance.

Ed adds: Thanks to my agent Matt Wagner for again turning me into a *Dummies* author. It is a privilege to be working with you once more. I'd also like to thank Jim Henderson, Geri Tucker, Nancy Blair and the rest of my *USA TODAY* friends and colleagues (in and out of the Money section) for your enormous support and encouragement. Most of all, thanks to my loving family for understanding my nightly (and weekend) disappearances as we raced to get this project completed on time.

And finally, thanks to you, gentle reader, for buying our book.

Publisher's Acknowledgments

We're proud of this book; please send us your comments through our online registration form located at www.dummies.com/register/.

Some of the people who helped bring this book to market include the following:

Acquisitions, Editorial, and Media Development

Project Editor: Susan Pink

Sr. Acquisitions Editor: Bob Woerner

Copy Editor: Susan Pink

Technical Editor: Dennis Cohen

Editorial Manager: Jodi Jensen

Editorial Assistant: Amanda Foxworth

Sr. Editorial Assistant: Cherie Case

Cartoons: Rich Tennant (www.the5thwave.com)

Composition Services

Project Coordinator: Bill Ramsey

Layout and Graphics: Laura Campbell, Stephanie D. Jumper, Brent Savage, Alicia B. South, Christine Williams

Indexer: Johnna VanHoose Dinse

Anniversary Logo Design: Richard Pacifico

Special Help

Kevin Kirschner, Clint Lahnen, Shelley Lea

Publishing and Editorial for Technology Dummies

Richard Swadley, Vice President and Executive Group Publisher

Andy Cummings, Vice President and Publisher

Mary Bednarek, Executive Acquisitions Director

Mary C. Corder, Editorial Director

Publishing for Consumer Dummies

Diane Graves Steele, Vice President and Publisher

Joyce Pepple, Acquisitions Director

Composition Services

Gerry Fahey, Vice President of Production Services

Debbie Stailey, Director of Composition Services

Contents at a Glance

Table of Contents

Introduction

*P*recious few products ever come close to generating the kind of buzz seen with the iPhone. Its messianic arrival received front-page treatment in newspapers and top billing on network and cable TV shows. People lined up days in advance just to ensure landing one of the first units. Years from now, people will insist, "I was one of them."

But we trust you didn't pick up this book to read yet another account about how the iPhone launch was an epochal event. We trust you *did* buy the book to find out how to get the very most out of your remarkable new device.

Our goal is to deliver that information in a light and breezy fashion. We expect you to have fun using your iPhone. We equally hope you will have fun spending time with us.

About This Book

Let's get one thing out of the way right from the get-go. We think you're pretty darn smart for buying a *For Dummies* book. That says to us you have the confidence and intelligence to know what you don't know. The Dummies franchise is built around the core notion that all of us feel insecure about certain topics when tackling them for the first time, especially when those topics have to do with technology.

As with most products coming out of Apple, the iPhone is beautifully designed and intuitive to use. And though our editors may not want us to reveal this dirty little secret (especially on the first page, for goodness sakes), the truth is you'll get pretty far just by exploring the iPhone's many functions and features on your own, without the help of this or any other book.

Okay, now that we spilled the beans, let's tell you why you shouldn't run back to the bookstore and request a refund. This book is chock full of useful tips, advice, and other nuggets that should make your iPhone experience all the more pleasurable. So keep this book nearby and consult it often.

Conventions Used in This Book

So let's tell you how we go about our business. *iPhone For Dummies* makes generous use of numbered and bulleted lists and pictures. Web addresses are shown in a special monofont typeface, `like this`.

We've also included a few sidebars with information that is not required reading (not that any of the book is) but that we hope will provide a richer understanding of certain subjects. Overall, we aim to keep technical jargon to a minimum, under the guiding principle that with rare exceptions you need not know what any of it really means.

How This Book Is Organized

Here's something we imagine you've never heard before: Most books have a beginning, middle, and end, and you'll do well by adhering to that linear structure. Unless you're one of those knuckleheads out to ruin it for the rest of us by revealing Harry Potter's fate.

Fortunately, there is no ending to spoil in a *For Dummies* book. So while you may well want to digest this book from start to finish — and we hope you do — we won't penalize you for skipping ahead and jumping around. Having said that, we organized *iPhone For Dummies* in an order that we think makes the most sense, as follows.

Part 1: Getting to Know Your iPhone

In the introductory chapters of Part I, you tour the iPhone inside and out, find out how to activate the phone with Apple's partner AT&T, and get hands-on (or, more precisely, fingers-on) experience with the iPhone's unique virtual multitouch display.

Part 11: The Mobile iPhone

There's a reason the iPhone has *phone* in its name. Part II is mostly about all the ways you can make and receive calls on the device. But you'll also discover how to exchange text messages and play with the Calendar, Clock, and Calculator applications.

Part 111: The Multimedia iPhone

Part III is where the fun truly begins. This is the iPhone as an iPod, meaning music, videos, movies, pictures, and other diversions come to life.

Part 1V: The Internet iPhone

Part IV covers the mobile Internet. You'll master the Safari browser, e-mail, maps, and more.

Part V: The Undiscovered iPhone

In Part V you find out how to apply your preferences through the iPhone's internal settings as well as discover where to go for troubleshooting assistance if and when the iPhone starts misbehaving.

Part VI: The Part of Tens

Otherwise known as the Dummies answer to David Letterman. The lists presented in Part VI steer you to terrific iPhone-related Web sites, provide handy tips and shortcuts, and offer our own suggestions on how you're newly favored device might get even better.

Icons Used in This Book

Little round pictures (icons) appear in the left margins throughout this book. Consider these icons miniature road signs, telling you a little something extra about the topic at hand or really hammering a point home.

Here's what the four different icons used in this book look like and mean.

These are the juicy morsels, shortcuts, and recommendations that might make the task at hand faster or easier.

This tip emphasizes the stuff we think you ought to retain. You may even jot down a note to yourself in the iPhone.

Put on your propeller beanie hat and pocket protector; this text includes the truly geeky stuff. You can safely ignore this material, but if it weren't interesting or informative, we wouldn't have bothered to write it.

You wouldn't intentionally run a stop sign, would you? In the same fashion, ignoring warnings may be hazardous to your iPhone and (by extension) your wallet. There, you now know how these warning icons work, for you have just received your very first warning!

Where to Go from Here

Why straight to Chapter 1, of course, (without passing Go).

In all seriousness, we wrote this book for you, so please let us know what you think. If we screwed up, confused you, left something out, or heaven forbid made you angry, drop us a note. And if we hit you with one pun too many, it helps to know that as well.

Since writers are people too (believe it or not), we also encourage positive feedback if you think it is warranted. So kindly send e-mail to Ed at baigdummies@aol.com and to Bob at iPhoneLeVitus@boblevitus.com. We'll do our best to respond to reasonably polite e-mail in a timely fashion.

Most of all, we want to thank you for buying our book. Please enjoy it along with your new iPhone.

Note: At the time we wrote this book, we covered the only iPhone model that was available and the latest version of iTunes. Apple is likely to introduce a new iPhone model or new version of iTunes between book editions. If you've bought a new iPhone or your version of iTunes looks a little different, be sure to check out the companion Web site (www.dummies.com/go/iphone1e) for updates on the latest releases from Apple.

Part I
Getting to Know
Your iPhone

*Y*ou have to crawl before you walk, so consider this part basic training for crawling. The three chapters that make up Part I serve as a gentle introduction to your iPhone.

We start out nice and easy, with a big-picture overview. In Chapter 1 we look at what's in the box. Then we examine just some of the cool things your iPhone can do. We finish things off with a quick-and-dirty tour of the hardware and the software.

Next, after you're somewhat familiar with where things are and what they do, we move right along to a bunch of useful iPhone skills, such as turning the darn thing on and off (which is very important) and locking and unlocking your phone (which is also very important). Chapter 2 ends with useful tips and tricks to help you master iPhone's unique multitouch interface so you can use it effectively and efficiently.

Then, in Chapter 3, we explore the process of synchronization and how to get data — contacts, appointments, movies, songs, podcasts, and such — from your computer into your iPhone quickly and painlessly.

Unveiling the iPhone

In This Chapter

➤ Looking at the big picture

➤ Touring the outside of the iPhone

➤ Checking out the iPhone's applications

Congratulations. You've selected one of the most incredible handheld devices we've ever seen — and one that is much more than just a great wireless phone. Of course, the iPhone is one heck of a wireless telephone, complete with a capable 2-megapixel digital camera. But it's actually three awesome handheld devices in one. In addition to being a killer cell phone, it's a gorgeous widescreen video iPod and the smallest, most powerful Internet communications device yet.

In this chapter, we offer a gentle introduction to all three "products" that make up your iPhone, plus overviews of its revolutionary hardware and software features.

The Big Picture

The iPhone has many best-of-class features, but perhaps its most unusual feature is the lack of a physical keyboard or stylus. Instead, it has a 3½-inch super-high-resolution touchscreen (160 pixels per inch if you care about such things) that you operate using a pointing device you're already intimately familiar with: namely, your finger.

And what a display it is. We venture that you've never seen a more beautiful screen on a handheld device in your life.

Bob interjects:

I am rarely tongue-tied but I could barely form coherent sentences during my first encounter with a real live iPhone at Macworld Expo last January. In fact, I had to explain to the Apple executives conducting my briefing, VP of Worldwide iPod Product Marketing Greg Joswiak and VP of Worldwide Mac Product Marketing David Moody, that while I knew it was completely unprofessional for a journalist to gush and drool, I just couldn't help myself.

Another feature that knocked our socks off was the iPhone's built-in sensors. An accelerometer detects when you rotate the device from portrait to land-scape mode and adjusts what's on the display accordingly. A proximity sensor detects when the iPhone gets near your face, so it can turn off the display to save power and prevent accidental touches by your cheek. And a light sensor adjusts the display's brightness based on the current ambient lighting situation. Let's see your Palm Treo or RIM Blackberry do *that!*

In this section we take a brief look at just some of the iPhone's features, broken down by product category.

What's in the box

Somehow we think you've already opened the handsome black box that the iPhone came in. But if you didn't, here's what you can expect to find inside:

- **Stereo headset:** Used for music videos and, yes, phone calls. The headset contains a built-in microphone for making yourself heard during phone calls. More on the use of this headset in Chapter 7.

- **Dock (and dock connector–to–USB cable):** When the iPhone is not being used, slip it into this handy little white home to charge it. The dock connects to your PC or Macintosh via USB through the aptly named dock connector–to–USB cable.

- **USB power adapter:** You can use the afore-mentioned cable to plug the iPhone into a standard power outlet.

- **Some Apple logo decals:** Of course.

- **Cleaning cloth:** Expect the iPhone to get smudges on it. Use the cloth to wipe it clean. We'd steer clear of Lemon Pledge.

- **Finger Tips pamphlet:** You'll find handy tips from Apple on using the new object of your affection.

- **Important Product Information Guide pamphlet:** Well it must be important because it says so right on the cover. You'll find basic safety warnings, a bunch of legalese, warranty information, and info on how to dispose of or recycle the iPhone. *What! We're getting rid of it already?* A few other pieces of advice: Don't drop the iPhone if you can help it, keep the thing dry, and — as with all cell phones — give full attention to the road while driving.

- **iPhone:** You were starting to worry. Yes, the iPhone itself is also in the box.

The iPhone as a phone and a digital camera

On the phone side, the iPhone synchronizes with the contacts and calendars on your Mac or PC. It includes a full-featured QWERTY soft, or virtual, keyboard, which makes typing text easier than ever before — for some folks. Granted, the virtual keyboard takes a bit of time to get used to. But we think that many of you will eventually be whizzing along at a much faster pace than you thought possible on a mobile keyboard of this type.

The 2-megapixel digital camera is accompanied by a sophisticated photo management application, so taking and managing digital photos is a pleasure rather than the nightmare it can be on other phones. Plus, you can automatically synchronize iPhoto photos with the digital photo library on your Mac or PC.

Finally, one of our favorite phone accoutrements is visual voicemail. (Try saying that three times fast.) This feature lets you see a list of voicemail messages and choose which ones to listen to or delete without being forced to take in every message in your voice mailbox in sequential order. Now that's handy!

Those are merely a few of the iPhone's excellent telephony features. Because we still have many more chapters to go, we'll put the phone coverage on hold for now (pun intended).

The iPhone as an iPod

We agree with Steve Jobs on this one: The iPhone is a better iPod than any that Apple has ever made. (Okay, we can quibble about wanting more storage.) You can enjoy all of your existing iPod content — music, audiobooks, audio and video podcasts, music videos, television shows, and movies — on the iPhone's gorgeous high-resolution color display, which is bigger, brighter, and richer than any iPod display that's come before it.

Bottom line: If you can get the content — be it video, audio, or whatever — into iTunes on your Mac or PC, you can synchronize it and watch or listen to it on your iPhone.

The iPhone as an Internet communications device

But wait — there's more! Not only is the iPhone a great phone and a stellar iPod, it's also a full-featured Internet communications device with — we're about to drop a bit of industry jargon on you — a rich HTML e-mail client that's compatible with most POP and IMAP mail services. Also on board is a world-class Web browser (Safari) that, unlike other phones, makes Web surfing fun and easy.

Another cool Internet feature is Maps, a killer mapping application based on Google Maps. You can view maps and satellite imagery and obtain driving directions and traffic information regardless of where in the United States you happen to be. You can also find businesses such as gas stations, restaurants, hospitals, and Apple stores with just a few taps.

You might also enjoy using Stocks, a built-in application that delivers near real-time stock quotes and charts anytime and anyplace.

In other words, the Internet experience on an iPhone is far superior to the Internet experience on any other handheld device.

Technical specifications

One last thing before we proceed. Here's a list of everything you need before you can actually *use* your iPhone:

- An iPhone (D'oh!)
- A wireless contract with AT&T (formerly Cingular)
- Internet access (required) or broadband Internet access (recommended)

Plus you need one of the following:

- A Mac with a USB 2.0 port; Mac OS X version 10.4.10 or later; and iTunes 7.3 or later
- A PC with a USB 2.0 port; Windows Vista Home Premium, Business, Enterprise, or Ultimate Edition or Windows XP Home or Professional with Service Pack 2 or later; and iTunes 7.3 or later

A Quick Tour Outside

The iPhone is a harmonious combination of hardware and software, so let's see just what it's made of. In this section we take a brief look at what's on the outside. In the next section, we peek at the software.

On the top

On the top of your iPhone, you'll find the headset jack, the SIM card tray, and the Sleep/Wake button, as shown in Figure 1-1:

- **The Sleep/Wake button:** This button is used to lock or unlock your iPhone and to turn your iPhone on or off. When your iPhone is locked, you can still receive calls and text messages but nothing happens if you touch its screen. When your iPhone is turned off, all incoming calls go directly to voicemail.

- **SIM card tray:** The SIM card tray is where you remove or replace the SIM card inside your iPhone.

  A SIM (Subscriber Identity Module) card is a removable smart card used to identify mobile phones. It allows users to change phones by moving the SIM card from one phone to another.

- **Headset jack:** The headset jack lets you plug in the included iPhone headset, which looks a lot like white iPod earbuds. Unlike the iPod earbuds, however, the iPhone headset has a microphone so you can use it to talk as well as to listen.

  The headset jack is recessed, so most third-party earphones (such as those made by Shure, Etymotic, and Future Sonics) don't work with it. Fortunately, for around $11 (at press time), you can buy an adapter from companies such as Belkin that enables you to use just about any brand or style of earphones you like with your iPhone.

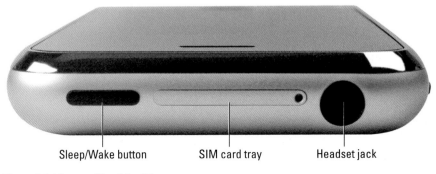

Sleep/Wake button   SIM card tray   Headset jack

Figure 1-1: The top side of the iPhone.

On the bottom

On the bottom of your iPhone, you'll find the speaker, dock connector, and microphone, as shown in Figure 1-2:

- **Speaker:** The speaker is used by the iPhone's built-in speakerphone and plays audio — music or video soundtracks — if no headset is plugged in. It also plays the ringtone you hear when you receive a call.

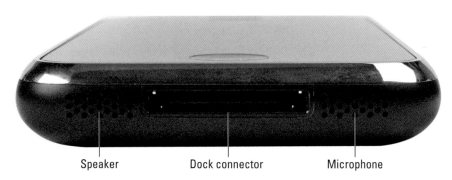

Speaker   Dock connector   Microphone

Figure 1-2: The bottom side of the iPhone.

✔ **Dock connector:** The dock connector has two purposes. One, you can use it to recharge your iPhone's battery. Simply connect one end of the included dock connector–to–USB cable to the dock connector and the other end to the USB power adapter. Two, you can use the dock connector to recharge your iPhone's battery as well as synchronize. Connect one end of the same cable to the dock connector and the other end to a USB port on your Mac or PC.

✔ **Microphone:** The microphone lets callers hear your voice when you're not using a headset.

On the front

On the front of your iPhone you'll find the following (labeled in Figure 1-3):

✔ **Ring/Silent switch:** The Ring/Silent switch, which is on the left side of your iPhone, lets you quickly switch between ring mode and silent mode. When the switch is set to ring mode — the up position, with no orange dot — your iPhone plays all sounds through the speaker on the bottom. When the switch is set to silent mode — the down position, with an orange dot visible on the switch — your iPhone doesn't make a sound when you receive a call or when an alert pops up on the screen. The only exceptions are alarms you set in the built-in Clock application, which do sound regardless of the Ring/Silent switch setting.

If your phone is set to ring mode and you want to silence it quickly, you can press the Sleep/Wake button on the top side of the iPhone or press one of the Volume buttons.

✔ **Volume buttons:** Two Volume buttons are just below of the Ring/Silent switch. The upper button increases the volume, the lower one decreases it. You use the Volume buttons to raise or lower the loudness of the ringer, alerts, sound effects, songs, and movies. And during phone calls, they adjust the loudness of the person you're speaking with, regardless of whether you're listening through the receiver, the speakerphone, or a headset.

✔ **Receiver:** The receiver is the speaker that the iPhone uses for telephone calls. It naturally sits close to your ear whenever you hold your iPhone in the "talking on the phone" position.

You should be the only one who hears sound coming from the receiver. If you have the volume set above about 50 percent and you're in a location with little or no background noise, someone standing nearby may be able to hear the sound too. So be careful.

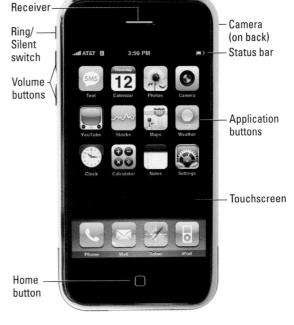

Figure 1-3: The front of the iPhone is a study in elegant simplicity.

If you require privacy during phone calls, the headset is a better bet.

✔ **Touchscreen:** You find out how to use the iPhone's gorgeous high-resolution color touchscreen in Chapter 2. All we have to say at this time is try not to drool all over it.

✔ **Home button:** No matter what you're doing, you can press the Home button at any time to display the Home screen, which is the screen shown in Figure 1-3.

✔ **Application buttons:** Each of the sixteen buttons launches an iPhone application. You'll read more about them later in this chapter and throughout the rest of the book.

On the back

On the back of your iPhone is the camera lens. It's the little circle in the top-left corner. For more on the camera, see Chapter 9.

Status bar

The status bar, which is at the top of the screen, displays tiny icons that provide a variety of information about the current state of your iPhone:

✔ **Cell signal:** The cell signal icon tells you whether you're within range of the AT&T cellular network and therefore can make and receive calls. The more bars you see (five is the highest), the stronger the cellular signal. If you're out of range, the bars are replaced with the words *No service.*

If you have only one or two bars, try moving around a little bit. Even moving just a few feet can sometimes mean the difference between no service and three or four bars.

✔ **Airplane mode:** You're allowed to use your iPod on a plane after the captain gives the word. But you can't use your cell phone except when the plane is in the gate area before takeoff or after landing. Fortunately, your iPhone offers an airplane mode, which turns off all wireless features of your iPhone — the phone, Internet access, Wi-Fi, and Bluetooth — and makes it possible to enjoy music or video during your flight.

✔ **Wi-Fi:** If you see the Wi-Fi icon, it means your iPhone is connected to the Internet over a Wi-Fi network. The more semicircular lines you see (up to three), the stronger the Wi-Fi signal. Once again, if you have only one or two bars of Wi-Fi strength, try moving around a bit. If you don't see the Wi-Fi icon in the status bar, Internet access is not currently available.

✔ **EDGE:** This icon tells you that AT&T's EDGE network is available and you can use it to connect to the Internet. If you don't see the EDGE icon in the status bar, Internet access is not currently available.

✔ **Lock:** This icon tells you when your iPhone is locked. See Chapter 2 for information on locking and unlocking your iPhone.

✔ **Play:** This icon informs you that a song is currently playing. You find out more about playing songs in Chapter 7.

✔ **Alarm:** This icon tells you that you have set one or more alarms in the Clock application.

✔ **Bluetooth:** This icon indicates the current state of your iPhone's Bluetooth connection. If it's blue, Bluetooth is on and a device (such as a wireless headset or car kit) is connected. If the icon is gray, Bluetooth is turned on but no device is connected. If you don't see a Bluetooth icon, Bluetooth is turned off. More on this in Chapter 15.

✔ **Battery:** This icon reflects the level of your battery's charge. It's completely filled when your battery is fully charged, and then empties out as your battery becomes depleted. You'll see a lightning bolt inside it when your iPhone is recharging.

The iPhone's Sweet Sixteen

The Home screen displays sixteen icons, each representing a different application or function. Because the rest of the book covers all of them in greater detail, we merely provide brief descriptions here.

Starting at the top left, the applications on your Home screen are as follows:

- **Text:** The Text application lets you exchange text messages with almost any other cell phone user. We've used a lot of mobile phones in our day and this application is as good as it gets.

- **Calendar:** No matter what calendar program you prefer on your PC or Mac (as long as it's iCal, Microsoft Entourage, or Microsoft Outlook), you can synchronize events and alerts between your computer and your iPhone. Create an event on one and it's automatically synchronized with the other the next time they're connected. Neat stuff.

- **Photos:** This application is the iPhone's terrific photo manager. You can view pictures that you take with the iPhone's built-in camera or photos transferred from your computer. You can zoom in or out, create slideshows, e-mail photos to friends, and much more. Other phones may let you take pictures; the iPhone lets you enjoy them in many ways.

- **Camera:** Use this application when you want to shoot a picture with the iPhone's fine 2-megapixel camera.

- **YouTube:** This application lets you watch videos from the popular YouTube Web site. You can search for a particular video or browse through thousands of offerings. It's a great way to waste a lot of time.

- **Stocks:** If you follow the market, this application lets you monitor your favorite stocks, which are updated in near real time.

- **Maps:** This application is among our favorites. View street maps or satellite imagery of locations around the globe, or ask for directions, traffic conditions, or even the location of a nearby pizza joint. The only thing that would make it even better would be GPS.

- **Weather:** This application monitors the six-day weather forecast for as many cities as you like.

- **Clock:** This program lets you see the current time in as many cities as you like, set one or more alarms for yourself, and use your iPhone as a stopwatch or a countdown timer.

- **Calculator:** The Calculator application lets you perform addition, subtraction, multiplication, and division. Period.

- ✓ **Notes:** This program lets you type notes while you're out and about. You can send the notes to yourself or anyone else through e-mail or just save them on your iPhone until you need them.

- ✓ **Settings:** Use this application to adjust your iPhone's settings. If you're a Mac user, think System Preferences; if you're a Windows person, think Control Panel.

- ✓ **Phone:** Tap this application icon to use the iPhone as a phone. What a concept!

- ✓ **Mail:** This application lets you send and receive e-mail with most POP3 and IMAP e-mail systems.

- ✓ **Safari:** Safari is your Web browser. If you're a Mac user, you know that already; if you're a Windows user, think Internet Explorer on steroids.

- ✓ **iPod:** Last but not least, this icon unleashes all the power of a video iPod right on your phone.

Okay then. Now that you and your iPhone have been properly introduced, it's time to turn it on, activate it, and actually use it. Onward!

Basic Training

The last time you bought a cell phone, the process probably went something like this: You wandered into a wireless store unsure what you wanted. You checked out a few models in your price range and chose one that met your budget, feature requirements, and sense of style. You waited patiently while the friendly (we hope) salesperson recorded some vital information and eventually activated the phone.

By now, of course, you know that the iPhone is a very different deal. Amidst extraordinary buzz, you plotted for months about how to land one. After all, the iPhone is the ultimate fashion phone, and the chic device also hosts a bevy of cool features. (Keep reading this book for proof.) To snatch the very first version, you may have had to save your pennies — or at least said "the budget be damned." Owning the hippest and most hyped handset on the planet comes at a premium cost compared with rival devices.

Something else is different about the iPhone purchasing experience: the way it's activated. No salesperson is going to guide you through the process, whether you picked up your newly prized possession in an Apple retail store, an AT&T retail store, or on the Web. Instead, you are supposed to handle activation solo, in the comfort of your own home.

©iStockphoto.com/DRabPics

Fortunately, as with most products with an Apple pedigree, the process of getting up to speed with the iPhone is dirt simple and fun. Although hiccups are possible — just ask some of the folks who bought an iPhone in the days following its June 29, 2007 debut — activation should go smoothly. If you do need assistance, let this chapter be your guide.

Turning the iPhone On and Off

Apple has taken the time to partially charge your iPhone, so you'll get some measure of instant gratification. After taking it out of the box, press and hold the Sleep/Wake button on the top-right edge. (Refer to Chapter 1 for the location of all buttons.) The famous Apple logo should show up on your screen, followed a few seconds later by a stunning image of Earth.

Not so subtle message: Apple has ambitious aspirations about capturing global market share.

The words *Activate iPhone* appear at the top of the screen above the home planet, accompanied by a message to *Connect to iTunes*.

You are permitted at this initial stage to make an emergency call by using your finger to slide the arrow at the bottom of the display to the right. It's a bit startling to see the emergency option on this early screen. Here's hoping that your first act as an iPhone owner will not land you or a loved one in the hospital.

To turn the device completely off, press and hold the Sleep/Wake button again until a red arrow appears at the top of the screen. Then drag the arrow to the right with your finger.

Locking the iPhone

A naked cell phone in your pocket is asking for trouble. Unless the phone has some locking mechanism, you may inadvertently dial a phone number. Try explaining to your boss why he or she got a call from you at 4 A.M. Fortunately, Apple makes it a cinch to lock the iPhone so that this scenario won't happen to you.

In fact, you don't need to do anything to lock the iPhone; it happens automatically, as long as you don't touch the screen for a minute.

Can't wait? To lock the iPhone immediately, press the Sleep/Wake button. To unlock it, press the Sleep/Wake button again. Or press the Home button on the front of the screen, and then drag the onscreen slider to the right with your finger.

By now you're picking up on the idea that your fingers play an important role in controlling your iPhone. We talk more about the role your digits play later in this chapter.

Activating the iPhone

There are two prerequisites for enjoying the iPhone. First, you have to become or already be an AT&T (U.S.), T-Mobile (Germany), O2 (U.K.), or Orange (France) customer. Read the sidebar titled "The Great Escape: Bailing out of your wireless contract," later in this chapter, if you are in the middle of a contract with a rival wireless phone company.

Second, make sure you download the latest version of iTunes software onto your PC or Mac. Apple doesn't supply the software in the box, so head to www.apple.com/itunes if you need to fetch a copy or launch your current version of iTunes, and choose Check for Updates. You'll find it under the Help menu on a Windows machine and the iTunes menu on a Mac.

For the uninitiated, iTunes is the nifty Apple jukebox software that iPod owners and many other people use to manage music, videos, and more. iTunes is at the core of the iPhone as well, because an iPod is built into the iPhone. You'll employ iTunes to synchronize a bunch of stuff on your computer and iPhone: contacts, calendars, e-mail accounts, bookmarks, photos, videos, and of course music. And from the get-go, you'll use iTunes to activate the phone.

Here's how to proceed with setup:

1. **Locate an available USB port on your PC or Mac to connect the dock. Slide the iPhone into its dock.**

   Hold your excitement as the first *Welcome to Your New iPhone* greeting is displayed inside iTunes, as shown in Figure 2-1.

2. **Click Continue to get on with the show.**

3. **Select whether or not you are already an AT&T (or Cingular) wireless customer, and then click Continue.**

   The screen displayed in Figure 2-2 appears.

Figure 2-1: Welcome to the iPhone, you lucky dog.

Figure 2-2: Requesting or renewing your AT&T credentials.

4. **Based on the decision in Step 3, select among the following options. Then click Continue.**

   If you're in the AT&T stable, you can either add a new line to an existing account or replace your current phone with the iPhone. If you're an AT&T newbie, you can activate either a single iPhone or — you'd be the envy of your neighborhood — two or more iPhones under a family plan.

5. **(Optional) You have the option of transferring an existing cell phone number from another wireless provider to the iPhone, a process that Apple says may take up to six hours.**

   If you want to do so, select the Transfer Existing Mobile Number box and fill in your existing phone number, account number, zip code, and account password (if applicable). There are plenty of good reasons for keeping your old number, not least of which is to brag to friends that they're calling you on an iPhone. Although you'll be able to make outgoing calls at this juncture, you won't be able to receive any until the transfer is complete. Then proceed with Step 7.

6. **Click Continue.**

7. **Choose your monthly wireless plans from AT&T, and then click Continue.**

   Figure 2-3 shows the most common options for voice minutes and text messages as of this writing. Click the arrow next to More Minutes to check out higher-priced plans. Click Less Minutes to return to the lower-priced options.

   Pay heed to the fine print. You better learn to love AT&T because, for better or worse, they're going to be your wireless carrier for at least the next two years. The iPhone is not compatible with Verizon Wireless, Sprint, or any other US carrier.

8. **If you have an Apple ID, type your Apple ID and password. Then click Continue.**

9. **Enter your date of birth and select the appropriate boxes if you want to receive e-mail on new releases and additions to the iTunes Store or special offers and information about other Apple products. Then click Continue.**

10. **Well, you knew they would get around to it sooner or later. In the next screens, enter your billing address and acknowledge that you have read both Apple's iPhone Terms & Conditions and AT&T's Service Agreement (if you're new to AT&T). Click Continue to move from screen to screen.**

    I don't know anyone without a law degree who actually reads these things. But high up in the AT&T agreement you learn that you're subject to a $175 early termination fee should you decide to bail out of your contract. Ouch!

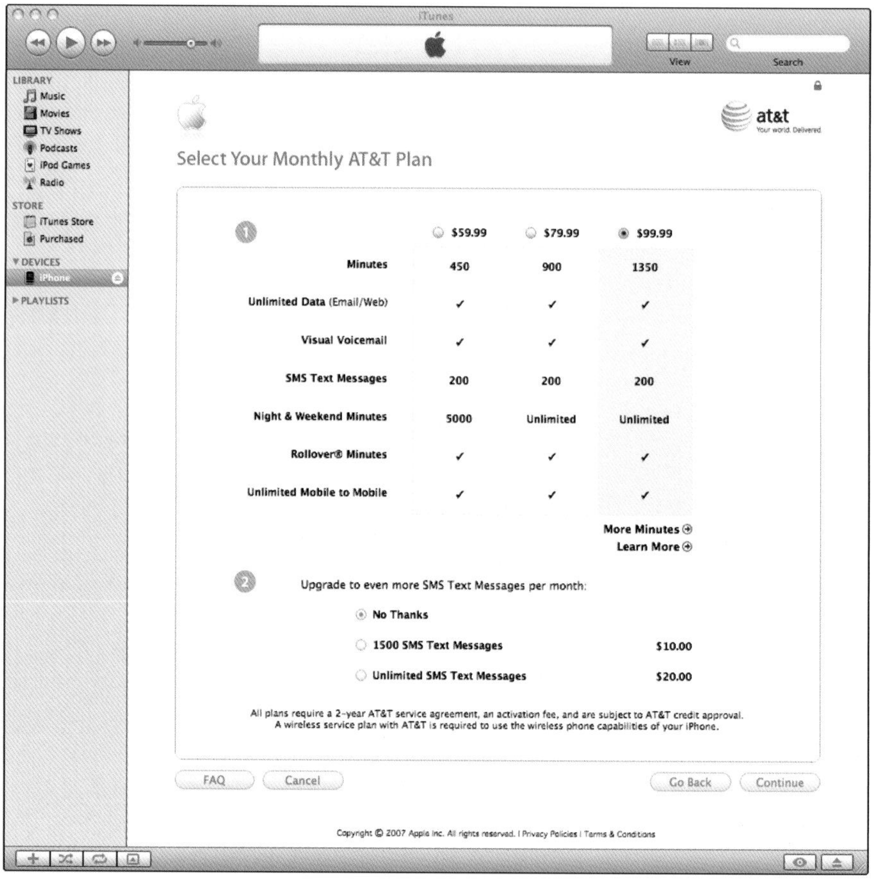

Figure 2-3: Choosing your minutes.

11. You get one more shot to review your information. If your address and the iPhone plan are accurate, click Submit to authorize AT&T to perform a credit check and initiate service (again, if you're new to AT&T).

Click Go Back to make changes. Processing the activation could take up to three minutes, assuming there are no snags.

TIP

If you don't pass the credit check, all is not lost. As this book was being prepared, AT&T was offering a prepaid plan for the iPhone (though the rates are not as attractive). The plan is not available to customers whose credit is A-OK.

The Great Escape: Bailing out of your wireless contract

In most instances, a wireless provider will sell you a deeply discounted phone or even issue you a free model. But there's one expensive catch. You're subject to hefty termination fees if you bail out of your (typical) two-year contract early.

The iPhone is one Cingular . . . make that AT&T sensation (bad pun intended), so you'll have to wave sayonara to Sprint, Verizon, or other carriers if you want a device. But breaking a cell phone contract is not easy, and some of the options for doing so may not be quite the outs you had in mind: You can enlist in the military, move overseas, even die. (But then AT&T's coverage may not reach heaven.)

Fortunately, there are other options, though none are guaranteed to work:

✐ **Complain loudly and often:** If you've been having problems with your existing carrier, contact the phone company and tell them how lousy your coverage is. Document your complaints in writing and be as specific as possible about spots where your calls drop out.

✐ **Keep an eye out for price hikes:** If the carrier ups rates dramatically on text messaging, say, you may have a legal out in your contract. The `Consumerist.com` Web site advises you to read any notices of changes to your Terms of Service that come your way. These may void the original agreement and you'll have about a month to cancel your contract.

✐ **Use online matchmaking:** Sites such as `www.celltradeusa.com` and `www.cell swapper.com` are in the business of matching users who want to get out of their contract with other folks who are seeking a bargain. The person trying to ditch a contract pays a modest fee to these sites. The motivation for the person who takes the contract off your hands? They need not pay an activation fee to the carrier and have no long-term commitment of their own.

✐ **Roam, roam on the range:** If you keep using your phone outside your carrier's network, it may become uneconomical for *them* to want to keep you. That's because your phone company picks up expensive roaming charges.

12. **If all is peachy, your new mobile number, assuming you didn't keep your old one, is displayed on the computer screen.**

   Meanwhile, the iPhone will notify you when activation is complete and send an e-mail to the address you designated.

13. **Click Continue to begin syncing your iPhone with your contacts, calendars, e-mail accounts, bookmarks, music, photos, and pictures.**

   Skip ahead to the next chapter for details on syncing.

Mastering the Multitouch Interface

Virtually every cell phone known to mankind has a physical (typically plastic) dialing keypad, if not also a more complete QWERTY-style keyboard, to bang out e-mails and text messages. The iPhone dispenses with both. Apple is once again living up to an old company advertising slogan to "Think Different."

Indeed, the iPhone removes the usual physical buttons in favor of a so-called *multitouch display.* It is the heart of many things you do on the iPhone, and the controls change depending on the task at hand.

Unlike other phones with touchscreens, don't bother looking for a stylus. You are meant, instead — to lift another ancient ad slogan — to "let your fingers do the walking."

The first thing to note is that there are actually three keyboard layouts: the alphabetical keyboard, the numeric and punctuation keyboard, and the more punctuation and symbols keyboard. All three are shown in Figure 2-4.

Figure 2-4: The three faces of the iPhone keyboard.

There are four keys that don't actually type a character: the Shift, Toggle, Delete, and Return keys:

- **Toggle key:** Switches between the different keyboard layouts.

- **Shift key:** If you're using the alphabetical keyboard, the Shift key switches between uppercase and lowercase letters. If you're using either of the other two keyboards, pressing Shift switches to the other one.

To turn on Caps Lock and type in all caps, you first need to enable Caps Lock. You do that by tapping the Settings icon, then tapping General, and then tapping Keyboard. Tap the Enable Caps Lock item to turn it on. Once the Caps Lock setting is enabled (it's disabled by default), you double-tap the Shift key to turn on Caps Lock. (The Shift key turns blue whenever Caps Lock is on.) Tap the Shift key again to turn off Caps Lock. To disable Caps Lock completely, just reverse the process by turning off the Enable Caps Lock setting (tap Settings, General, Keyboard).

- **Delete key:** Erases the character immediately to the left of the cursor.

If you hold down the Delete key for a few seconds, it begins erasing entire words rather than individual characters.

- **Return key:** Moves the cursor to the beginning of the next line.

The incredible, intelligent, and virtual iPhone keyboard

Before we consider how to actually *use* the keyboard, we'd like to share a bit of the philosophy behind its so-called intelligence. Knowing what makes this keyboard smart will help you make it even smarter when you use it:

- It has a built-in English dictionary that even includes words from today's popular culture.

- It adds your contacts to its dictionary automatically.

- It uses complex analysis algorithms to predict the word you're trying to type.

- It suggests corrections as you type. It then offers you the suggested word just below the misspelled word. When you decline a suggestion and the word you typed is *not* in the iPhone dictionary, the iPhone will add that word to its dictionary and offer it as a suggestion if you mistype it in the future.

Remember to decline suggestions — doing so helps your intelligent keyboard become even smarter.

✔ It reduces the number of mistakes you make as you type by intelligently and dynamically resizing the touch zones for certain keys. You can't see it, but it is increasing the zones for keys it predicts might come next and decreasing the zones for keys that are unlikely or impossible to come next.

Training your digits

Rice Krispies has Snap! Crackle! Pop! Apple's response for the iPhone is Tap! Flick! and Pinch! Yikes, another ad comparison.

Fortunately, tapping, flicking, and pinching are not challenging gestures, so you'll be mastering many of the iPhone's features in no time:

✔ **Tap:** Tapping serves multiple purposes, as will become evident throughout this book. You can tap an icon to open an application from the Home screen. Tap to start playing a song or to choose the photo album you want to look through. Sometimes you will double-tap (tapping twice in rapid succession), which has the effect of zooming in (or out) of Web pages, maps, and e-mails.

✔ **Flick:** Just what it sounds like. A flick of the finger on the screen itself lets you quickly scroll through lists of songs, e-mails, and picture thumbnails. Tap on the screen to stop scrolling or merely wait for the scrolling list to stop.

✔ **Pinch:** Place two fingers on the edges of a Web page or picture to enlarge the images or make them smaller. Pinching is a cool gesture that is easy to master and sure to wow an audience. If you need practice, visit the Apple iPhone blogs at `www.theiphoneblogs.com/2007/ 01/12/practice-your-apple-iphone-pinch/`.

Finger-typing

Apple's multitouch interface just might be considered a stroke of genius. And it just might as equally drive you nuts, at least initially.

If you're patient and trusting, you'll get the hang of finger-typing in a week or so. You have to rely on the virtual keyboard (which appears when you tap a text field) to enter notes, compose text messages, type the names of new contacts, and so forth.

Apple's own recommendation — which we concur with — is to start typing with just your index finger before graduating to two thumbs.

Fingers or thumbs?

There is one last thing: Should you use your fingers or thumbs to type? The answer is: Both. It seems somewhat easier to hold the iPhone in your nondominant hand (that is, your left hand if you're right handed or vice versa) and type with the index finger of your dominant hand, especially when you're first starting out with the iPhone. And that's what we suggest you try first.

Later, when you get the hang of typing with one index finger, you can try to speed things up by using both hands. There are two possible ways you can do it:

✔ Set the iPhone on a sturdy surface (such as a desk or table) and tap with both index fingers. Some users prefer this technique. But

you can't easily use it when you're standing up with no sturdy surface of the proper height available.

✔ Cup the iPhone with both hands and type with both thumbs. This technique has the advantage of being possible in almost any situation with or without a sturdy surface. The downside is that your thumbs are bigger than your fingers so it takes more practice to type accurately with them.

Which is better? Don't ask us — try it both ways and use the method that feels the most comfortable or lets you type with the best accuracy. Better still, master both techniques and use whichever is more appropriate at the time.

The good news is that Apple has built a lot of intelligence into its virtual keyboard, so it can correct typing mistakes on-the-fly and take a stab at predicting what you are about to type next. The keyboard isn't exactly Nostradamus, but it does a pretty good job in coming up with the words you have in mind.

As you press your finger against a letter or number on the screen, the individual key you press gets bigger and practically jumps off the screen, as shown in Figure 2-5. That way, you know that you struck the correct letter or number.

Alas, mistakes are common at first. Say you meant to type a sentence in the Notes application that reads, "I am typing a bunch of notes." But because of the way your fingers struck the virtual keys, you actually entered "I am typing a bunch of *npyrs*. Fortunately, Apple knows that the *o* you meant to press is next to the *p* that showed up on the

Figure 2-5: The ABC's of virtual typing.

keyboard, just as *t* and *y* and the *e* and the *r* are side-by-side. So the software determines that *notes* was indeed the word you had in mind and places it in red under the suspect word, as shown in Figure 2-6. To accept the suggested word, merely tap the Space key. And if for some reason you actually did mean to type *npyrs* instead, tap on the suggested word (*notes* in this example) to decline it.

Moreover, because Apple knows what you are up to, the virtual keyboard is fine-tuned for the task at hand. If you're entering a Web address, for example, the keyboard inside the Safari Web browser (see Chapter 10) includes dedicated period, forward slash, and .com keys but no Space key. If you're using the Notes application (see Chapter 5), the keyboard does have a Space key. And if you're composing an e-mail message, a dedicated @ key pops up on the keyboard.

When you're typing notes or sending e-mail and want to type a number, symbol, or punctuation mark, you have to tap the *.?123* key to bring up an alternative virtual keyboard. Tap the *ABC* key to return to the first keyboard. It's not hard to get used to, but some may find this extra step irritating.

Editing mistakes

It's a good idea to type with reckless abandon and not get hung up over the characters you mistype. Again, the self-correcting keyboard will indeed fix many errors. That said, plenty of typos will likely turn up, especially in the beginning, and you'll have to make corrections manually.

A neat trick for doing so is to hold your finger against the screen to bring up the magnifying glass shown in Figure 2-7. Use it to position the pointer to the spot where you need to make the correction.

There, you've survived basic training. Now the real fun is about to begin.

Figure 2-6: When the keyboard bails you out.

Figure 2-7: Magnifying errors.

The Kitchen Sync: Getting Stuff to and from Your iPhone

In This Chapter

▷ Starting your first sync

▷ Disconnecting during a sync

▷ Synchronizing contacts, calendars, e-mail accounts, and bookmarks manually

▷ Synchronizing music, podcasts, video, and photos

*W*hen you have activated your iPhone and have passed basic training (in Chapter 2), the next thing you're likely to want to do is get some or all of your contacts, appointments, events, mail settings, bookmarks, music, movies, TV shows, podcasts, and photos into your iPhone.

We have good news and . . . more good news. The good news is that you can easily copy any or all of those items from your computer to your iPhone. And the more good news is that once you do that, you can synchronize your contacts, appointments, and events so they are kept up-to-date automatically in both places — on your computer and your iPhone — whenever you make a change in one place or the other. So when you add or change an appointment, an event, or a contact on your iPhone, that information automatically appears on your computer the next time your iPhone and computer get together.

©iStockphoto.com/ronen

This process is called syncing (short for synchronizing) your iPhone and computer. Don't worry: It's easy, and we're going to walk you through the entire process in this chapter.

But wait. There's even more good news. Items you manage on your computer — such as music, movies, TV shows, podcasts, photos, and e-mail account settings — are synchronized only one way: from your computer to your iPhone, which is the way it should be.

Starting to Sync

Synchronizing your iPhone with your computer is a lot like syncing an iPod with your computer. If you're an iPod user, the process will be a piece of cake. But it's not too difficult even for those who've never used an iPod:

1. **Start by connecting your iPhone to your computer using the dock and the dock connector–to–USB cable, both of which were in the box with your iPhone.**

   Technically, the dock is optional. You can just plug the dock connector on the cable into your iPhone. Synchronization (and recharging) will work perfectly either way, so it's up to you.

   When you connect your iPhone to your computer, iTunes should launch automatically. If it doesn't, chances are you plugged the cable into a USB port on your keyboard, monitor, or hub. Try plugging it into one of the USB ports on your computer instead. Why? Because USB ports on your computer supply more power to a connected device than USB ports on a keyboard, monitor, or most hubs.

   If iTunes still doesn't launch automatically, try launching it manually.

   One last thing: If you've taken any photos with your iPhone since the last time you synced it, your photo management software (iPhoto on the Mac; Adobe Photoshop Album or Elements on the PC) will launch and ask if you want to import the photos from your phone. You'll find out all about this later in the chapter.

2. **Select your iPhone in the iTunes source list.**

   You see the Set Up Your iPhone pane, as shown in Figure 3-1.

   If you don't see an iPhone in the source list, and you're sure it's connected to a USB port on your computer (not the keyboard, monitor, or hub), restart your computer.

3. **Name your iPhone.**

   We've cleverly named this one *MyiPhone.*

4. **Decide whether you want iTunes to automatically synchronize your iPhone and your contacts, calendars, e-mail accounts, and bookmarks.**

   • If that's what you want, just select the check box, click Done, and continue with the "Synchronizing Your Media" section.

   • If you want to synchronize manually, click Done. The "Synchronizing Your Data" section tells you all about how to configure your contacts, calendars, e-mail accounts, and bookmarks manually.

   We've chosen to not select the check box because this computer has four e-mail accounts and we don't want all of them to synchronize with the iPhone.

iPhone selected in source list

Figure 3-1: This is the first thing you'll see in iTunes.

After you click the Done button, the Summary pane should appear. If it doesn't, make sure your iPhone is still selected in the source list and click the Summary tab near the top of the window, as shown in Figure 3-2.

Figure 3-2: The Summary pane is pretty painless.

5. **If you want iTunes to sync your iPhone automatically whenever you connect it to your computer, select the Automatically Sync When This iPhone Is Connected check box (in the Options area).**

    Don't select it if you want to sync manually by clicking the Sync button at the bottom of the window.

6. **If you want to sync only items that are selected in your iTunes library, select the Only Sync Checked Items check box.**

Your choice in Step 5 not set in stone. If you select the Automatically Sync When This iPhone Is Connected check box, you can still prevent your iPhone from syncing automatically in several different ways:

- **Way #1:** After you connect the iPhone to your computer, click the Summary tab in iTunes and then deselect Automatically Sync When This iPhone Is Connected. This will also prevent iTunes from opening automatically when you connect the iPhone. If you use this method, you can still start a sync manually.

- **Way #2:** Launch iTunes, and then before you connect your iPhone to your computer, press and hold Command+Option (Mac) or Shift+Control (PC) until you see your iPhone in the iTunes source list. This method prevents your iPhone from syncing automatically just this one time, without changing any settings.

And, of course, if you uncheck the Automatically Sync When This iPhone Is Connected check box, you can always synchronize manually by clicking the Summary tab and then clicking the Sync button in the bottom-right corner of the window.

By the way, if you've changed any sync settings since the last time you synchronized, the Sync button will instead say Apply.

Disconnecting the iPhone

When the iPhone is syncing with your computer, its screen says *Sync in progress* and iTunes displays a message that says it's syncing with your iPhone. When the sync is finished, iTunes displays a message that the iPhone sync is complete and it's okay to disconnect your iPhone.

If you disconnect your iPhone before a sync is completed, all or part of the sync may fail.

To cancel a sync so you can safely disconnect your iPhone, drag the slider on the iPhone (the one that says *Slide to Cancel*) during the sync.

If you get a call while you're syncing, the sync is canceled automatically so you can safely disconnect your iPhone and answer the call. When you're finished with the call, just reconnect your iPhone to restart the sync.

Synchronizing Your Data

Did you choose to set up data synchronization manually (by not selecting the Automatically Sync Contacts, Calendars, Email Accounts, and Bookmarks check box in the Set Up Your iPhone pane shown in Figure 3-1)? If so, your next order of business is to tell iTunes what data you want to synchronize between your iPhone and your computer. You do this by clicking the Info tab, which is to the right of the Summary tab.

The Info pane has five sections: Contacts, Calendars, Mail Accounts, Web Browser, and Advanced. Let's take a look at them one by one.

Contacts

The Contacts section of the Info pane determines how synchronization is handled for your contacts. One method is to synchronize all of your contacts, as shown in Figure 3-3. Or you can synchronize any or all groups of contacts you've created in your computer's address book program; just click the appropriate check boxes and only those groups will be synchronized.

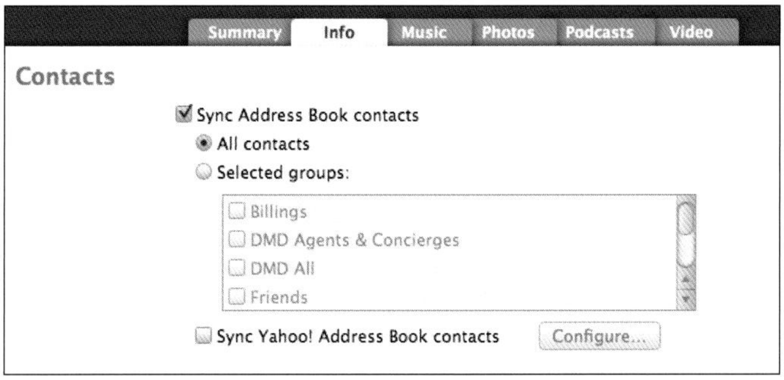

Figure 3-3: Want to synchronize your contacts? This is where you set things up.

The iPhone syncs with the following address book programs:

- **Mac:** Address Book and other address books that sync with Address Book, such as Microsoft Entourage and Yahoo! Address Book
- **PC:** Yahoo! Address Book, Windows Address Book (Outlook Express), and Microsoft Outlook

If you use Yahoo! Address Book, click Configure to enter your Yahoo! ID and password. Also, syncing will never delete a contact from your Yahoo! Address Book if it has a Messenger ID, even if you delete that contact on the iPhone or on your computer.

To delete a contact that has a Messenger ID, log in to your Yahoo! account with a Web browser and delete the contact in Yahoo! Address Book.

Calendars

The Calendars section of the Info pane determines how synchronization is handled for your appointments and events. You can synchronize all of your calendars, as shown in Figure 3-4. Or you can synchronize any or all individual calendars you've created in your computer's calendar program. Just click the appropriate check boxes.

| Summary | **Info** | Music | Photos | Podcasts | Video |

Calendars

☑ Sync iCal calendars
   ◉ All calendars
   ○ Selected calendars:

   ☐ Bob's Appointments
   ☐ Bob's Travel
   ☐ Bob's Deadlines
   ☐ Family

☑ Do not sync events older than 30 days

Put new events created on this iPhone into the calendar: [Bob's Appointm... ◆]

Figure 3-4: Set up sync for your calendar events here.

The iPhone syncs with the following calendar programs:

  ✔ **Mac:** iCal, plus any tasks or events that currently sync with iCal on your Mac, such as events and tasks in Microsoft Entourage

  ✔ **PC:** Microsoft Outlook

One cool thing about syncing your calendar is that if you create reminders, alerts, or alarms in your computer's calendar program, they appear (and sound) on your iPhone at the appropriate date and time.

Mail accounts

You can sync account settings for your e-mail accounts in the Mail Accounts section of the Info pane. You can synchronize all of your e-mail accounts (if you have more than one), or you can synchronize individual accounts as shown in Figure 3-5. Just click the appropriate check boxes.

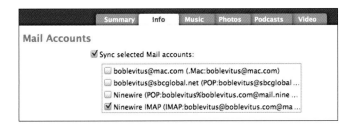

Figure 3-5: Transfer e-mail account settings to your iPhone here.

The iPhone syncs with the following mail programs:

- ✓ **Mac:** Mail and Microsoft Entourage
- ✓ **PC:** Microsoft Outlook and Microsoft Outlook Express

E-mail account settings are synchronized only one way: from your computer to your iPhone. If you make changes to any e-mail account settings on your iPhone, the changes will *not* be synchronized back to the e-mail account on your computer. Trust us, this is a very good feature and we're glad Apple did it this way.

By the way, the password for your e-mail account may or may not be saved on your computer. If you sync an e-mail account and the iPhone asks for a password when you send or receive mail, do this: Tap Settings on the Home screen, tap Mail, tap your e-mail account's name, and then type your password in the appropriate field.

Web browser

The Web Browser section has but a single check box, which asks if you want to sync your bookmarks. Select it if you do; don't select it if you don't.

The iPhone syncs bookmarks with the following Web browsers:

- ✓ **Mac:** Safari
- ✓ **PC:** Microsoft Internet Explorer and Safari

Advanced

Every so often the contacts, calendars, mail accounts, or bookmarks on your iPhone get so screwed up that the easiest way to fix things is to erase that information on your iPhone and replace it with information from your computer.

If that's the case, just click the appropriate check boxes, as shown in Figure 3-6. Then the next time you sync, that information on your iPhone will be replaced with information from your computer.

| Summary | Info | Music | Photos | Podcasts | Video |

Advanced

Replace information on this iPhone:
- [ ] Contacts
- [ ] Calendars
- [ ] Mail Accounts
- [ ] Bookmarks

During the next sync only, iTunes will replace the selected information on this iPhone with information from this computer.

Figure 3-6: Replace the information on your iPhone with the information on your computer.

Because the Advanced section is at the bottom of the Info pane and you have to scroll down to see it, it's easy to forget that it's there. Try not to. Although you probably won't need to use this feature very often (if ever), you'll be happy you remembered that it's there if you do need it.

Synchronizing Your Media

If you're among the readers who chose to let iTunes manage synchronizing their data automatically, welcome back. Now let's look at how you get your media — your music, podcasts, video, and photos — from your computer to your iPhone.

Music, podcasts, and video (but not photos) are synced only one way: from your computer to your iPhone. Deleting any of these items from your iPhone will not delete them from your computer when you sync.

Music, podcasts, and video

You use the Music, Podcasts, and Video panes to specify the media that you want to copy from your computer to your iPhone. To view any of these panes, make sure that your iPhone is still selected in the source list and then click the Music, Podcasts, or Video tab near the top of the window.

Music

To transfer music to your iPhone, select the Sync Music check box in the Music pane. Then you can choose all songs and playlists or only selected playlists. You can also choose to include music videos. See Figure 3-7.

Music

☑ Sync music
  ○ All songs and playlists
  ● Selected playlists:

  ☐ Purchased
  ☐ A 45 Day Playlist
  ☐ A Music Only Playlist
  ☐ A One Year Music Playlist
  ☑ A Six Month Music Playlist
  ☐ Brits w/o Beatles
  ☐ Elvis the C
  ☐ Great Gig
  ☐ My Top Rated
  ☐ Recently Played
  ☐ Top 100 Most Played
  ☐ 'tis the season...
  ☐ Amy Winehouse – Back to Black
  ☐ Bob LeVitus's Playlist
  ☐ Bob's Nano

☑ Include music videos

Figure 3-7: Use the Music pane to copy music from your computer to your iPhone.

If you choose All Songs and Playlists and have more songs in your iTunes library than storage space on your iPhone — just over 7GB on an 8GB iPhone — you'll see one or both of the error messages shown in Figure 3-8 when you try to sync.

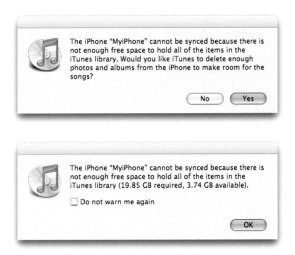

Figure 3-8: If you have more music than your iPhone has room for, this is what you'll see when you sync.

To avoid these errors, select playlists that total less than 3 or 7 gigabytes.

Music, podcasts, and video are notorious for chewing up massive amounts of storage space on your iPhone. If you try to sync too much media, you'll see lots of error messages like the ones in Figure 3-8. Forewarned is forearmed.

Podcasts

To transfer podcasts to your iPhone, select the Sync check box in the Podcasts pane. Then you can choose all podcasts or only selected playlists, as shown in Figure 3-9.

Summary	Info	Music	Photos	**Podcasts**	Video

Podcasts

☑ Sync [3 most recent   ⬍] episodes of:
○ All podcasts
◉ Selected podcasts:

- ● ☑ Coverville
- ☑ MacNotables
- ☑ Onion News Network (Video)
- ☐ PODRUNNER: Exercise music for running, spinnin ...
- ☑ Strong Bad Emails & More!
- ☐ Videos – Beginner Guitar Lessons and Songs by iPl ...

Figure 3-9: The Podcasts pane determines which podcasts will be copied to your iPhone.

Regardless of whether you choose to sync all podcasts or only selected podcasts, a pop-up menu allows you to specify which episodes you want to sync, as shown in Figure 3-10.

Summary	Info	Music	Photos	**Podcasts**	Video

Podcasts

☑ Sync
○ Al
◉ Se

all
1 most recent
3 most recent
5 most recent
10 most recent

all unplayed
1 most recent unplayed
3 most recent unplayed
5 most recent unplayed
10 most recent unplayed

all new
1 most recent new
3 most recent new
5 most recent new
10 most recent new

episodes of:

for running, spinnin ...

ions and Songs by iPl ...

Figure 3-10: This menu determines how podcasts are synced with your iPhone.

Video

To transfer TV shows and movies to your iPhone, select the appropriate check boxes in the Video pane, as shown in Figure 3-11.

Figure 3-11: Your choices in the Video pane determine which TV shows and movies are copied to your iPhone.

The procedure for syncing TV shows is slightly different from the procedure for syncing movies. First, select the Sync check box to enable TV show syncing. Then choose either All TV Shows or Selected. If you go with Selected, you can then choose between TV Shows and Playlists from the pop-up menu (which says TV Shows in Figure 3-11).

Next, choose how many episodes you want to sync from the pop-up menu shown in Figure 3-12 (which says 3 Most Recent Unwatched in Figure 3-11).

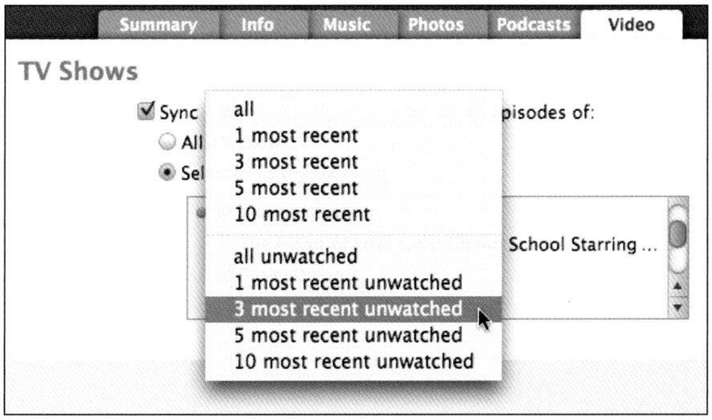

Figure 3-12: This menu determines how TV shows are synced with your iPhone.

To sync movies, you need to first select the Sync Movies check box, and then select the check boxes of the individual movies you want to sync.

Photos

Syncing photos is a little different from syncing other media because your iPhone has a built-in camera and you may want to copy pictures you take with the iPhone to your computer as well as copy pictures stored on your computer to your iPhone.

The iPhone syncs photos with the following programs:

- **Mac:** iPhoto version 4.03 or later, Aperture, and any folder that contains images
- **PC:** Adobe Photoshop Album 2.0 or later, Adobe Photoshop Elements 3.0 or later, and any folder that contains images

To sync photos, click the Photos tab near the top of the window. In the Photos pane, select the Sync Photos From check box and then choose an application or folder from the pop-up menu (which says iPhoto in Figure 3-13).

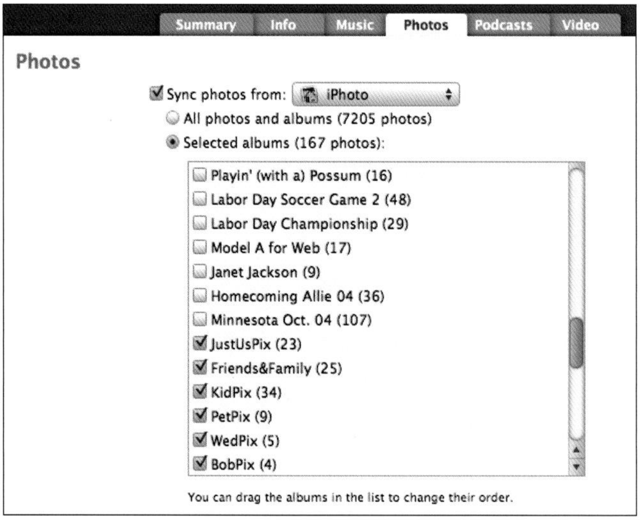

Figure 3-13: The Photos pane determines which photos will be synchronized with your iPhone.

If you choose an application that supports photo albums, as we have in Figure 3-13, you can select specific albums. If you choose a folder full of images, you can create subfolders inside it which will appear as albums on your iPhone. But if you choose an application that doesn't support albums, or a single folder full of images (with no subfolders), it's all or nothing.

You can rearrange the album list by clicking an album name and dragging it up or down in the list.

If you've taken any photos with your iPhone since the last time you synced it, the appropriate program will launch (or the appropriate folder will be selected) and you'll have the option of downloading the pictures to your computer. The process is the same as when you download pictures from your digital camera.

How much space did I use?

If you're interested in knowing how much free space is available on your iPhone, look near the bottom of the iTunes window while your iPhone is selected in the source list. You'll see a chart that shows the contents of your iPhone, color-coded for your convenience. As you can see in Figure 3-14, this 8GB iPhone has roughly 3.73GB of free space available.

Figure 3-14: This handy chart tells you how much space is being used on your iPhone.

The chart appears at the bottom of the iTunes window regardless of which pane is currently selected.

For those who are wondering, Other is the catchall category for contacts, calendars, appointments, events, bookmarks, and e-mail stored on your phone. In our case, the total of these items is a mere 37MB, a tiny fraction of the total storage space available on this iPhone.

Part II
The Mobile iPhone

The 5th Wave   By Rich Tennant

CELL PHONES

"Of course your iPhone lets you watch videos, listen to music, and surf the Web. But does it shoot silly string?"

*Y*our iPhone is first and foremost a mobile phone, so in this part we explore how to use typical mobile phone features, starting with all the neat ways to make an outgoing phone call. You also find out how to answer or ignore the calls that come in and discover iPhone's clever visual voicemail feature, which lets you take in messages on your terms, rather than in the order in which the messages arrived on the phone. You also figure out how to juggle calls, merge calls, and decide on a ringtone.

Then, after you've mastered all the calling and listening stuff, you are ready to become a whiz at sending and retrieving what are called SMS text messages. As journalists, we especially appreciate what comes next: finding out how to become a champion note-taker.

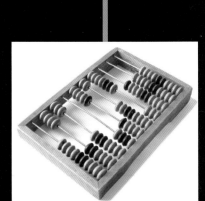

We close this part by investigating all those C-word programs — namely, Calendar, Calculator, and Clock. These handy applications not only enable you to solve arithmetic problems on-the-fly, but also help you stay on top of your appointments and — thanks to a built-in alarm clock — show up for them on time.

Understanding the
Phone-damentals

*Y*ou may well have bought an iPhone for its spectacular photo viewer, marvelous widescreen iPod, and the best darn pocket-size Internet browser you'll ever come across. Not to mention its overall coolness.

For most of us, though, cool goes only so far. The iPhone's most critical mission is the one from which its name is derived — it is first and foremost a cell phone. And no matter how capable it is at all those other things, when push comes to shove you had best be able to make and receive phone calls.

That puts a lot of responsibility in the hands of AT&T (formerly Cingular Wireless), the iPhone's exclusive wireless carrier. As with any cell phone, the strength of the wireless signal depends a great deal on your location and the robustness of the carrier's network.

As noted in Chapter 1, the cell signal status icon at the upper-left corner of the screen can clue you in on what your phone calling experience may be like. Simply put, more bars equates to a better experience. What you hope to avoid are those two dreaded words, *No Service.*

©iStockphoto.com/kledge

Cell coverage aside, this chapter is devoted to all the nifty ways to handle wireless calls on an iPhone.

Somewhere Alexander Graham Bell is beaming.

Making a Call

Start by tapping the Phone icon on the Home screen. You can then make calls by tapping on any of the icons that show up at the bottom of the screen: Favorites, Recents, Contacts, Keypad, or Voicemail. Depending on the circumstances, one of these could be the most appropriate method. Let's take them one by one.

Contacts

If you read the chapter on syncing (Chapter 3), you know how to get the snail-mail addresses, e-mail addresses, and (most relevant for this chapter) phone numbers that reside on your PC or Mac into the iPhone. Assuming you went through that drill already, all those addresses and phone numbers are hanging out in one place. Their not-so-secret hiding place is revealed when you tap the Contacts icon inside the Phone application.

Here's how to make those contacts work to your benefit:

1. **Inside the Phone application, tap Contacts.**

2. **Flick your finger so that the list of contacts on the screen scrolls rapidly up or down, loosely reminiscent of the spinning Lucky 7s (or other pictures) on a Las Vegas slot machine.**

   Think of the payout you'd get with that kind of power on a One-Armed Bandit.

   Alternatively, you can tap one of the teeny-tiny letters to the right side of your Contacts list to jump to names that begin with that letter.

3. **When you're at or near the appropriate contact name, stop the scrolling by tapping the screen.**

   Note that when you tap to stop the scrolling, that tap doesn't select an item in the list. That may seem counterintuitive the first few times you try it, but we got used to it and now we really like it this way.

4. **Tap the name of the person you want to call.**

   As shown in Figure 4-1, you'll notice a bunch of fields with the individual's phone numbers, physical and e-mail addresses, and possibly even their mug.

And since odds are pretty good that the person has more than one phone number, the hardest decision you must make is choosing which of those to call. When you've reached a decision, tap the number, and the iPhone initiates the call.

Your own iPhone phone number, lest you forget it, is always shown at the top of the Contacts list.

You can also initiate text messages and e-mails from within Contacts. Those topics are discussed in greater depth in Chapters 5 and 11, respectively.

Favorites

Consider Favorites the iPhone equivalent of speed dialing. It's where you can keep a list of the people and numbers you dial most often. Merely tap the person's name in Favorites and your iPhone calls the person.

Figure 4-1: Contact me.

You can set up as many favorites as you need for a person. So, for example, you may create separate favorites listings for your spouse's office phone number and cell number.

Setting up favorites is a breeze. You may have noticed a button on the Contacts screen labeled Add to Favorites. When you tap that button, all the phone numbers you have for that person pop up. Tap the number you want to make a favorite and it will turn up on the list.

You can rearrange the order in which your favorites are displayed. Tap Edit, and then, to the right of the person you want to move, press your finger against the symbol that looks like three short horizontal lines stacked on top of one another. Drag that symbol to the place on the list where you want your favorite contact to appear.

You can designate new favorites from within the Favorites application by tapping on the + symbol at the upper-right corner of the screen. Doing so brings you back to Contacts. From there, choose the appropriate person and number.

If one of your chosen folks falls out of favor, you can easily kick them off the Favorites roster. Here's how.

1. **Tap the Edit button in the upper-left corner of the screen.**

   You'll notice that a red circle with a horizontal white line appears to the left of each name in the list.

2. **Tap the circle next to the A-lister getting the heave-ho.**

   The horizontal white line is now vertical and a red Remove button appears to the right of the name, as shown in Figure 4-2.

3. **Tap Remove.**

   The person (or one of their given phone numbers) is no longer afforded the privilege of being in your iPhone inner circle.

Booting someone off the Favorites list does not remove them from the main Contacts list.

Figure 4-2: I don't like you anymore.

Recents

Tapping the Recents icon displays the iPhone call log. The Recents feature will house logs of all the, well, recent calls made or received, as well as calls that you missed. Here's a tricky concept: Tap All to show all the recent calls and Missed to show just those you missed. Under the All list, completed calls are shown in black and missed calls are in red.

By tapping the small blue circle with the right-pointing arrow next to the list, you can access information about the time a call was made or missed, as well as any known information about the caller from your Contacts information.

To return a call, just tap anywhere on the name.

If one of the calls you missed came from someone who isn't already in your Contacts, you can add him or her. Tap the right-pointing arrow, and then tap the Create New Contact button.

If the person is among your Contacts but has a new number, tap the Add to Existing Contact button.

When the list gets too long, tap Clear to clean it up.

Keypad

From time to time, of course, you have to dial the number of a person or company who hasn't earned a spot in your Contacts.

That's when you'll want to tap the keypad icon to bring up the large keys of the virtual touch-tone keypad you see in Figure 4-3. Despite what you may have read elsewhere, we find it surprisingly simple to manually dial a number on this keypad. Just tap the appropriate keys and tap Call.

About our only quibble is that you won't be able to dial without looking at the screen; dialing without looking is possible on at least some of the handsets with physical keypads.

You can use the iPhone's keypad also to remotely check your voicemail at work or home.

Come to think of it, what a perfect segue to the next section. It's on one of our favorite iPhone features, visual voicemail.

Figure 4-3: A virtually familiar way to dial.

Visual voicemail

How often have you had to listen to four or five (or more) voicemail messages before getting to the message you really want, or need, to hear? As shown in Figure 4-4, the iPhone's clever visual voicemail presents a list of your voicemail messages in the order in which calls were received. But you need not listen to those messages in order.

How do you even know you have a voicemail? There are a few ways:

- A red circle showing the number of pending messages awaiting your attention appears above the Phone icon on the Home screen, or above the Voicemail icon from within the Phone application.

- You may also see a message on the iPhone display that says something like, "New voicemail from Ed (or Bob)."

Whatever draws you in, tap that Voicemail icon to display the list of voicemails. You see the caller's phone number, assuming this info is known through CallerID, and in some cases his or her name. Or you see the word *Unknown*.

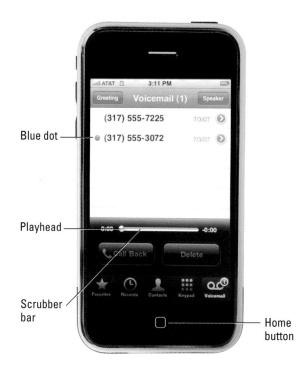

Blue dot

Playhead

Scrubber
bar

Home
button

Figure 4-4: Visual voicemail in action.

The beauty of all this, of course, is that you can ignore or at least put off listening to certain messages. We are not in the advice-giving business on what
calls you can safely avoid. In other words, ignore messages from the IRS or
your parole officer at your own risk.

A blue dot next to a name or number signifies that you haven't heard the
message yet.

To play back a voicemail, tap the name or number in question. Then tap the
tiny play/pause button that shows up to the left. Tap once more to pause the
message; tap again to resume. Tap the Speaker button if you want to hear the
message through the iPhone's speakerphone.

The tiny playhead along the scrubber bar (refer to Figure 4-4) shows you the
length of the message and how much of the message you've heard. If you
hate when callers ramble on forever, you can drag the playhead to rapidly
advance through a message. Perhaps more importantly, if you miss something, you can replay that segment.

Returning a call is as simple as tapping the green Call Back button. And you
can delete a voicemail by pressing Delete.

The globetrotting iPhone

Apple's device is a *quad-band GSM (850, 900, 1800, 1900 MHz) world phone.* Before you break into a sweat over the terminology, know that all we're really talking about is a phone you can use to make calls while traveling abroad. You'll have to have AT&T turn on something called international roaming. Contact AT&T for the latest rates, which were fairly harsh at the time this book was being prepared. Go to `www.wireless.att.com/learn/international` for details.

If you're calling the U.S. while overseas, you can take advantage of International Assist. It's a feature that automatically adds the proper prefix to U.S. numbers dialed from abroad. Tap Settings, Phone and then International Assist. Make sure you see the blue On button instead of the white Off button.

At least one company, Jajah, is providing a far cheaper workaround for making international calls from the U.S. (and elsewhere) with an iPhone. Check out `www.jajah.com` for the skinny.

If you have no phone service, you'll see a message that says *Visual Voicemail is currently unavailable.*

You can listen to your iPhone voicemail from another phone. Just dial your iPhone number and, while the greeting plays, enter your voicemail password. You can set up such a password by tapping Settings from the Home screen and then tapping Phone. Tap Change Voicemail Password. You'll be asked to enter your current voicemail password, if you already have one. If one doesn't exist yet, tap Done. If it does exist, enter it and then tap Done. You'll then be asked to type the new password and tap Done, twice.

Recording a greeting

You have two choices when it comes to the voicemail greeting your callers will hear. You can accept a generic greeting with your phone number by default. Or you can create a custom greeting in your own voice. The steps:

1. **Inside the voicemail application, tap the Greeting button.**

2. **Tap Custom.**

3. **Tap Record and start dictating a clever, deserving-of-being-on-the-iPhone voicemail greeting.**

4. **When you have finished recording, tap Stop.**

5. **Review the greeting by pressing Play.**

6. **If the greeting is worthy, tap Save. If not, tap Cancel and start over at Step 1.**

Receiving a Call

It's wonderful to have numerous options for making a call. But what are your choices when somebody calls you? The answer depends on whether you are willing to take the call or not.

Accepting the call

To accept a call, you have three options:

- Tap Answer and greet the caller in whatever language makes sense.
- If the phone is locked, drag the slider to the right.
- If you are donning the stereo earbuds that come with the iPhone, click the microphone button.

If you are listening to music in your iPhone's iPod when a call comes in, the song stops playing and you have to decide whether to take the call. If you do, the music will resume from where you left off once the conversation ends.

Rejecting the call

We're not going to assume that you are a cold-hearted person out to break a caller's heart. Rather, we assume that you are a busy person who will call back at a more convenient time.

Keeping that positive spin in mind, here are three ways to reject a call on the spot and send the call to voicemail:

- Tap Decline. Couldn't be easier than that.
- Press the Sleep/Wake button twice in rapid succession. (The button is on the top of the device.)
- Using the supplied headset, press and hold the microphone button for a couple of seconds and then let go. Two beeps let you know that the call was indeed rejected.

Sometimes you're perfectly willing to take a call but you need to silence the ringer or turn off the vibration. To do so, press the Sleep/Wake button a single time, or press one of the volume buttons. You'll still have the opportunity to answer.

Choosing ringtones

At the time this book was written, Apple included 25 ringtones in the iPhone, ranging from the sound of crickets to an old car horn. To choose a ringtone:

1. **From the Home screen, tap Settings.**

2. **Tap Sounds.**

3. **Tap Ringtone to access the list of available ringtones, shown in Figure 4-5.**

4. **Flick your finger to move up or down the list.**

5. **Tap any of the ringtones to hear what it will sound like.**

   A checkmark appears next to the ringtone you've just listened to.

6. **If satisfied, you need do nothing more. Unbeknownst to you, you have just selected that ringtone. If not pleased, try another.**

Figure 4-5: Ring my chimes: the iPhone's ringtones.

TIP

You can easily assign specific ringtones to individual callers. From Contacts, choose the person to whom you want to designate a particular ringtone. Tap Edit and then tap Assign Ringtone. This displays the aforementioned list of ringtones. Choose the one that seems most appropriate (a barking dog, say, for your father-in-law).

To change or delete the ringtone for a specific person, go back into Contacts, and tap Edit. Either tap the right arrow to choose a new ringtone for that person or tap the red circle and Delete to remove the custom ringtone altogether.

---

iTunes and ringtones

As of this writing, there is no way to turn the music in your iTunes library into custom ringtones. The hurdles aren't so much technical as economic — cell phone carriers charge a lot for ringtones — and it all boils down to who owns the digital rights to the music you thought was yours. You can buy ringtones from the iTunes Store for 99 cents each, but you need to pay the 99 cents even if you've already purchased the complete song. That doesn't seem quite fair to us, but that's the way it works.

While on a Call

You can do lots of things while talking on an iPhone, such as consulting your Calendar, taking notes, or checking the weather. Tap the Home button to get to these other applications. You've just witnessed the multitasking marvel that is the iPhone.

TIP

If you're using Wi-Fi, you can also surf the Web (through Safari) while talking on the phone. But you can't if your only outlet to cyberspace is the EDGE network.

Other options:

Figure 4-6: Managing calls.

- ✔ **Mute a call:** From the main call screen (shown in Figure 4-6) tap mute. Now you need not mutter under your breath when a caller ticks you off; they can't hear you. Tap mute again to un-mute the sound.

- ✔ **Tap contacts to display the Contacts list.**

- ✔ **Place a call on hold:** Again, pretty self-explanatory. Just tap hold. Tap hold again to take the person off hold. You might put a caller on hold to answer another incoming call or to make a second call yourself. The next section deals with more than one call at a time.

- ✔ **Tap keypad to bring back the keypad:** This is useful if you have to type touch-tones to access another voicemail system or respond to an automated menu system. Heaven forbid you actually get a live person when calling an insurance company or airline. But we digress . . .

- ✔ **Use the speakerphone:** Tap speaker to listen to a call through the iPhone's internal speakers without having to hold the device up to your mouth.

- ✔ **Make a conference call:** Read on.

Juggling calls

You can field a new call when you're already talking to somebody. Or ignore it (by tapping Ignore).

To take the new call while keeping the first caller on hold, tap the Hold Call + Answer button that appears, as shown in Figure 4-7. You can then toggle between calls (placing one or the other on hold) by tapping either the Swap button or the first call at the top of the screen.

If this is too much for you and that second caller is really important, tap End Call + Answer to ditch caller number one.

Merging calls

Now suppose caller number one and caller number two know each other. Or you'd like to play matchmaker so they get to know each other. Tap Merge Calls so all three of you can chitchat.

Conference calls

Now let's assume you have to talk to your whole sales team at once. It may be time to initiate a conference call, which effectively takes this merge call idea to its extreme. You can merge up to five calls at a time. In fact, creating such a conference call on the iPhone may be simpler than getting the same five people in a physical room at the same time.

Figure 4-7: Swapping calls.

Here's how you do it. Start by making a call and then placing the caller on hold as noted in "Juggling calls." Tap Add Call to make another call and then Merge Calls to bring everybody together. Repeat this exercise to add the other calls.

Other conference call tidbits:

- ✓ iPhone is actually a two-line phone, and one of the available lines can be involved in a conference call.

- ✓ If you want to drop a call from a conference, tap Conference and then tap the red circle with the little picture of the phone in it that appears next to the call. Tap End Call to make that caller go bye-bye.

✔ You can speak privately with one of the callers in a conference. Tap Conference, and then tap Private next to the caller you want to go hush-hush with. Tap Merge Calls to bring the caller back into the Conference so everyone can hear him or her.

✔ You can add a new incoming caller to an existing conference call by tapping Hold Call + Answer followed by Merge Calls.

There's even more you can do with iPhone the phone. Check out Chapter 13 for extra phone tips. Meanwhile, we recommend that you read the next chapter to figure out how to become a whiz at text messaging.

5

Texting 1, 2, 3: SMS Messages and Notes

In This Chapter

▶ Sending and receiving SMS text messages

▶ Using the Notes application

There has never been a device like the iPhone, so chances are this is your first experience with an intelligent virtual keyboard. In the beginning, it will probably feel awkward. Within a few days, however, many iPhone users report that they not only have become comfortable using it but have become proficient virtual typists as well.

By the time you finish this chapter we think you'll feel comfortable and proficient, too. You discover all about using the virtual keyboard in Chapter 2. In this chapter we focus on two of the iPhone applications that use text, namely Text (SMS) and Notes.

Texting

The Text application lets you exchange short text messages with any cell phone that supports the SMS protocol (which is almost all cell phones today).

SMS is the acronym for the Short Message Service protocol, often known as *text messaging* or just plain *texting*.

Typing text on a cell phone with a 12-key numeric keypad is an unnatural act, which is why many people have never sent a single SMS text message. The iPhone will change that. The intelligent virtual keyboard makes it easy to compose short text messages, and the big, bright, high-resolution screen makes it a pleasure to read them.

©iStockphoto.com/kutay tanir

But before we get to the part where you send or receive SMS messages, let's go over some SMS basics:

- Both sender and receiver need SMS-enabled mobile phones. Your iPhone qualifies, as does almost any mobile phone made in the past four or five years. Keep in mind that if you send SMS messages to folks with a phone that doesn't support SMS, they will never get your message nor will they know you even sent a message.

- Some phones (not the iPhone, of course) limit SMS messages to 160 characters. If you try to send a longer message to one of these phones, your message may be truncated or split into multiple shorter messages. The point is that it's a good idea to keep SMS messages brief.

- Most iPhone plans include 200 SMS text messages per month. If you use more than 200, you'll be charged extra for each message over 200.

  Each individual message in a conversation counts against this total even if it's only a one-word reply such as "OK," or "CUL8R" (which is teenager for "see you later").

- You can increase the number of SMS messages in your plan for a few more dollars a month. This is almost always less expensive than paying for them a la carte.

- You can send or receive SMS messages only over the AT&T network. Put another way, SMS messages can't be sent or received over a Wi-Fi connection.

Okay. Now that we have that out of the way, let's start with how to send SMS text messages.

You send me: Sending SMS text messages

Tap the Text (SMS) icon on the Home screen to launch the Text application, and then tap the little pencil and paper icon in the top-right corner of the screen to start a new text message.

At this point, the To field is active and awaiting your input. You could do three things at this point:

- If the recipient isn't in your Contacts list, type his or her cell phone number.

- If the recipient is in your Contacts list, type the first few letters of the name. A list of matching contacts appears. Scroll through it if necessary and tap the name of the contact.

TIP

The more letters you type, the shorter the list becomes.

✔ Tap the blue plus icon on the right side of the To field to select a name from your contact list.

There's a fourth option if you want to compose the message first and address it later. Tap the text entry field, which is just above the keyboard and to the left of the Send button, and type your message. When you've finished typing, you'll need to tap the To field and use one of the preceding techniques to address your message.

When you have finished addressing and composing, tap the Send button to send your message on its merry way. And that's all there is to it.

Being a golden receiver: Receiving SMS text messages

First things first. If you want to hear an alert sound when you receive an SMS text message, tap the Settings icon on your Home screen, tap Sounds, and then turn on the New Text Message item. (If you don't want to hear an alert when an SMS message arrives, turn it off.) Remember, though, that even if the New Text Message option is turned on, you won't hear any alert sound when an SMS message arrives if the Ring/Silent switch is off.

Two things happen when you receive an SMS text message. First, when you wake up your iPhone, all or part of the text will appear on the unlock screen. Second, after you unlock the phone, the Text icon on the Home screen displays the number of unread messages.

To read your message, tap the Text icon and the Text Messages screen appears. Tap the message to read it. If you want to reply to the message, tap the text entry field to the left of the Send button, and the keyboard appears. Type a reply and then tap Send.

Your conversation is saved as a series of text bubbles. Your messages appear on the right side of the screen in green bubbles; the other person's messages appear on the left in gray bubbles, as shown in Figure 5-1.

You can delete a conversation in two ways :

✔ **If you're viewing the conversation:** Tap the Clear button at the top right of the conversation screen.

✔ **If you're viewing the list of text messages:** Tap the Edit button at the top left of the Text Messages list, and then tap the red minus icon that appears next to the conversation.

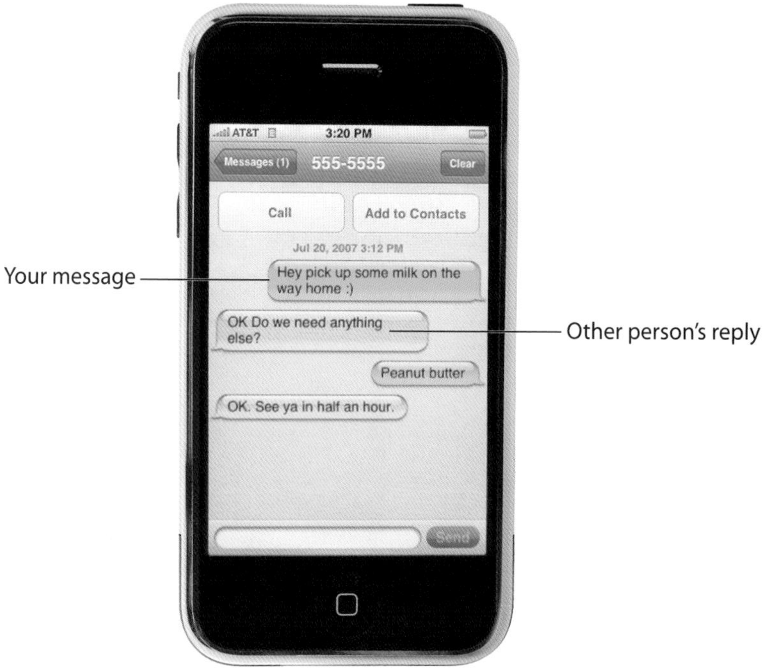

Figure 5-1: This is what an SMS conversation looks like.

Smart SMS tricks

Here are some more things you can do with SMS text messages:

- To send an SMS text message to someone in your Favorites or Recents list, tap the Phone icon on the Home screen, and then tap Favorites or Recents, respectively. Tap the blue > icon to the right of a name or number, and then tap Text Message at the bottom of the Info screen.

- To call or e-mail someone to whom you've sent an SMS text message, tap the Text icon on the Home screen, and then tap the message in the Text Messages list. Tap the Call button at the top of the conversation to call the person, or tap the Contact Info button and then tap an e-mail address to send an e-mail.

  You can use this technique only if the contact has an e-mail address.

- To add someone to whom you've sent an SMS text message to your Contacts list, tap their name or phone number in the Text Messages list and then tap the Add to Contacts button.

- ✔ If an SMS message includes a URL, tap it to open that Web page in Safari.
- ✔ If an SMS message includes a phone number, tap it to call that number.
- ✔ If an SMS message includes an e-mail address, tap it to open a pre-addressed e-mail message in Mail.
- ✔ If an SMS message includes a street address, tap it to see a map in Maps.

And that's all there is to it. You are now an official SMS text message maven.

Take Note of Notes

Notes is an application that creates text notes that you can save or send through e-mail. To create a note, first tap the Notes icon on the Home screen, and then tap the plus button in the top-right corner to start a new note. The virtual keyboard appears. Type the note. When you're finished, tap the Done button in the top-right corner to save the note. See Figure 5-2.

After a note is saved, you can do the following:

- ✔ Tap the Notes button at the top-left corner of the screen to see a list of all your notes. When the list is onscreen, just tap a note to open and view it.
- ✔ Tap the left or right arrow button at the bottom of the screen to read the previous or next note.
- ✔ Tap the letter button at the bottom of the screen to e-mail the note to someone with the Mail application (see Chapter 11).
- ✔ Tap the trash can button at the bottom of the screen to delete the note.

And that's all there is to it. You now know all there is to know about creating and managing notes with Notes.

Figure 5-2: The Notes application revealed.

6

Calendars and Calculators and Clocks, Oh My

In This Chapter

▷ Understanding the calendar's different views

▷ Calculating with your iPhone

▷ Using the clock as an alarm, a stopwatch, and a timer too

*T*he iPhone is a smartphone. And as a smart device it can remind you of appointments, tell you the time where you live or halfway around the world, and even solve simple arithmetic.

Over the next few pages we'll take a look at three of the iPhone's core — if frankly unsexy — applications. Indeed, we'd venture to say none of you actually bought an iPhone because of its calendar, calculator, or clock. Just the same, it's awfully handy having these programs around.

©iStockphoto.com/Baloncici

Working with the Calendar

The Calendar program lets you keep on top of your appointments and events (birthdays, anniversaries, and the like). You get there by tapping the Calendar icon on the Home screen. The icon is pretty smart in its own right because it changes daily; the day of the week and date are displayed.

You have three main ways to peek at your calendar: List, Day, and Month views. Choosing one is as simple as tapping on the List, Day, or Month button at the top of the Calendar screen. From each view, you can always return to the current day by tapping the Today button.

A closer look . . .

List view

Nothing complicated with the List view. As the name indicates, the List view, shown in Figure 6-1, presents current and future appointments in a list format. You can drag the list up or down with your finger. Or flick to rapidly scroll through the list. The List view pretty much compensates for the lack of a week-at-a-glance view, though Apple could certainly add such a feature, perhaps even by the time you read this book.

Frankly, we'd have loved for Apple to include multiple calendars, rather than just the single one here. A to-do list function would have also been nice. (Hey, nothing wrong with wanting more; in fact we devote Chapter 16 to our wish list.) You have our permission to lobby the gang in Cupertino.

If you're a Mac user who uses iCal, only part of this applies. You can create multiple calendars in iCal and choose which ones to sync with your phone (as described in Chapter 3).

Figure 6-1: The List view.

But be careful: To-do items created in iCal are not synced and won't appear on your iPhone. And even more unfortunately, all events from all of your iCal calendars show up on the single iPhone calendar after a sync.

Day view

The Day view, shown in Figure 6-2, reveals the appointments of a given 24-hour period (though you'll have to scroll up or down to see an entire day's worth of entries).

Month view

By now you're getting the hang of this. In Month view you can see appointments from January to December. In this monthly calendar view, you'll see a dot on any day that has appointments or events. Tap that day to see the list of activities that the dot represents. It's just below the month in view, as shown in Figure 6-3.

Figure 6-2: The Day view.

Figure 6-3: The Month view.

Adding Calendar Entries

In Chapter 3 you discover pretty much everything there is to know about syncing your iPhone. And that includes syncing calendar entries from your Windows machine (via the likes of Microsoft Outlook) or Mac (via iCal or Microsoft Entourage).

Of course, in plenty of situations you'll want to enter appointments on-the-fly. It's very easy to add appointments directly to the iPhone:

1. **Tap the Calendar icon at the top of the screen, and then tap the List, Day, or Month button.**

2. **Tap the + button at the upper-right corner of the screen.**

   The + appears whether you are in List, Day, or Month view. Tapping + displays the Add Event screen, shown in Figure 6-4.

3. **Tap the Title/Location field and finger-type as much or as little information as you feel is necessary.**

   Tapping displays the virtual keyboard.

4. **Tap Save.**

5. **If your calendar entry has a start time or end time (or both):**

   a. **Tap the Starts/Ends field.**

   b. **In the bottom half of the screen that appears (Figure 6-5), choose the time the event starts and then the time it ends.**

   Use your finger to roll separate wheels for the date, hour, minute (in 5-minute intervals), and AM or PM. It's a little like manipulating one of those combination bicycle locks.

   c. **Tap Save when you are finished.**

Figure 6-4: You are about to add an event to your iPhone.

6. **If you are entering a birthday or another all-day milestone, tap the All-day button so that On (rather than Off) is showing. Then tap Save.**

Since the time isn't relevant for an all-day entry, you'll note that the bottom half of the screen now has wheels for just the month, day, and year.

7. **If you are setting up a recurring entry, such as an anniversary, tap the Repeat window. Tap to indicate how often the event in question recurs, and then tap Save.**

The options are Every Day, Every Week, Every 2 Weeks, Every Month, Every Year.

8. **If you want to set a reminder or alert for the entry, tap Alert. Then tap on a time, and then tap Save.**

Alerts can be set to arrive on the actual date of an event, 2 days before, 1 day before, 2 hours before, 1 hour before, 30 minutes before, 15 minutes before, or 5 minutes before. At Alert time, you'll hear a sound and see a message like the one shown in Figure 6-6.

Are you the kind of person who needs an extra nudge? You can set another reminder by tapping on the Second Alert field.

9. **If you want to enter notes about the appointment or event, tap Notes. Type your note, and then tap Save.**

A virtual keyboard pops up so you can type in those notes.

10. **Tap Done when you have finished entering everything.**

Figure 6-5: Controlling the Starts and Ends fields is like manipulating a bike lock.

Figure 6-6: Alerts make it hard to forget.

You can turn off a calendar alert by tapping Settings, tapping Sounds, and then making sure the Calendar Alerts button is turned Off.

And if you want to modify an existing calendar entry, tap the entry, tap Edit, and then make whatever changes need to be made. To wipe out a calendar entry, tap Edit and then tap Delete Event. You'll get a chance to tap Cancel in case you tapped Delete Event by mistake.

Finally, calendar entries you create on your iPhone are synchronized with the calendar you specified in the iTunes Info pane.

Calculate This

Quick, what's 3467.8 times 982.3? Why the answer of course is 3406419.94.

We can solve the problem thanks to the iPhone's calculator, buried (until needed) under another of those Sweet Sixteen Home screen icons. Truth is, it's not the most advanced calculator you'll ever use. Go elsewhere for a sine or a square root. But for adding, subtracting, multiplying, and dividing, the iPhone calculator does just fine. Numbers and symbols (such as C for clear, and M+ for memory) are large and easy to see.

It's nice to know a smartphone can make you feel so much smarter.

Punching the Clock

We know what you must be thinking. "So the iPhone has a clock. Big deal. Doesn't every cell phone have a clock?"

Well, yes, every cell phone does have a clock. But not every phone has a "world clock" that lets you display the time in multiple cities on multiple continents. And not every cell phone has an alarm, a stopwatch, and a timer to boot.

Let's glance at those functions on your iPhone.

World clock

Want to know the time in Beijing or Bogota? Tapping on World Clock (inside the Clock application) lets you display the time in numerous cities around the globe, as shown in Figure 6-7.

Tap the + symbol at the upper-right corner of the screen and start typing a city name with the virtual keyboard. The moment you type the first letter, in fact, the iPhone displays a list of cities or countries that begin with that letter. So typing *V* will bring up both Vancouver, Canada and Caracas, Venezuela, among myriad other possibilities. You can create clocks for as many cities as you like, though the times in only four cities appear in a single screen. To see times in other cities, scroll up or down.

To remove a city from the list, tap Edit, and then tap the red circle with the white horizontal line in it to the left of the city you want to drop. Then tap Delete.

You can also rearrange the order of the cities displaying the time. Press your finger against the symbol with three horizontal lines to the right of the city you want to move up or down in the list and then drag it to its new spot.

Figure 6-7: What time is it in Budapest?

Alarm clock

Ever try and set the alarm in a hotel room? It's remarkable how complicated setting an alarm can be on even the most inexpensive clock radio. As with most things, the procedure is dirt simple on the iPhone:

1. **Tap Clock on the Home screen to display the Clock application.**

2. **Tap the Alarm icon at the bottom of the screen.**

3. **Tap the + sign at the upper-right corner of the screen.**

4. **Choose the time of the alarm by rotating the wheel on the bottom half of the screen.**

   This is similar to the action required to setting the time an event starts or ends in your calendar.

5. **If you want the alarm to go off on other days, tap Repeat and tell the iPhone the days you want the alarm to be repeated.**

6. **Tap Sound to choose the ringtone (see Chapter 4) that will wake you up.**

   This is a matter of personal preference, but we can tell you that the ringtone with the appropriate name Alarm managed to wake Ed out of a deep sleep.

7. **Tap Snooze to have the alarm appear on the screen accompanied by a Snooze button.**

   Tap the Snooze button to shut up the alarm for 10 minutes.

8. **If you want to call the alarm something other than, um, Alarm, tap the Label field and use the virtual keyboard to type another descriptor.**

9. **Tap Save when the alarm settings are to your liking.**

You'll know an alarm has been set and activated thanks to the tiny status icon — surprise, surprise, it looks like a clock — that appears in the upper-right corner of the screen.

An alarm will take precedence over any tracks you are listening to on the iPod. So songs will momentarily pause when an alarm goes off and resume when you turn off the alarm (or press the Snooze button).

Seems obvious, but to hear an alarm, make sure your iPhone's volume is turned up.

Stopwatch

If you're helping a loved one train for a marathon, your iPhone's Stopwatch function can provide an assist. It's accessible by tapping Stopwatch in the Clock application.

Just tap Start to begin the count and tap Stop at the finish line. You can also tap a Lap button to monitor the times between laps.

Timer

Cooking a hard-boiled egg or Thanksgiving turkey? Again, the iPhone comes to the rescue. Tap Timer (within the Clock app) and then rotate the hour and minute wheels until the time you have in mind is highlighted. Tap When Timer Ends to choose the ringtone that will signify that time's up.

After you've set up the length of the timer, tap Start when you're ready to begin. You can watch the minutes and seconds wind down on the screen if you have nothing better to do.

But you if you're doing anything else on the iPhone — admiring photos, say — you'll hear the ringtone and see a *Timer Done* message on the screen at the appropriate moment. Tap OK to silence the ringtone.

Now it's time to move on to the stuff that makes the iPhone really sexy.

Part III
The Multimedia iPhone

The 5th Wave By Rich Tennant

"Okay, the view's just up ahead. Everyone switch to 'America the Beautiful' on your iPhone playlist."

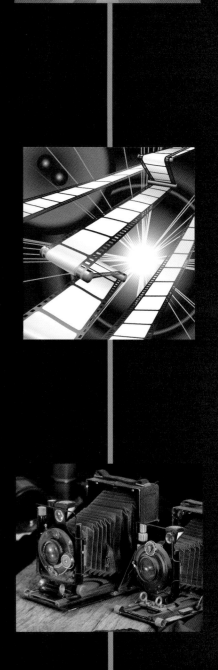

*Y*our iPhone is arguably the best iPod ever invented. So in this part we look at the multimedia side of your phone — audio, video, and still pictures, too. There has never been a phone that was this much fun to use; in this part we show you how to wring the most fun out of every multimedia bit of it.

First we explore how to enjoy listening to music, podcasts, and audiobooks on your iPhone. Then we look at some video, both literally and figuratively. We start off with a quick segment about how to find good video for your iPhone. We follow that with instructions for watching video on your iPhone.

Before we leave the video scene, you also see how to have a blast with video from the infamous YouTube Web site using iPhone's built-in YouTube application. We wrap this multimedia part up with everything you always wanted to know about photos and iPhones: how to shoot photos well, how to store them, how to sync them, and how to do all kinds of other interesting things with them.

Photo credits:
©iStockphoto.com/Kirsty Pargeter (Top)
©iStockphoto.com/Christos Georghiou (Middle)
©iStockphoto.com/Achim Prill (Bottom)

7

Get in Tune(s): Audio on Your iPhone

In This Chapter

▶ Introducing the iPod inside your iPhone

▶ Taking control of your tunes

▶ Customizing your audio experience

A s we mentioned elsewhere, your iPhone is also one heck of an iPod with video. In this chapter we show you how to use your iPhone for audio; in Chapter 8 we cover video.

We start with a quick tour of the iPhone's iPod application. Then we look at how to use your iPhone as an audio player. After you're nice and comfy with using it this way, we show you how to customize the listening experience so it's just the way you like it. Finally, we offer a few tips that will help you get the most out of using your iPhone as an audio player.

We're going to assume that you've synced your iPhone with your computer and that your iPhone contains audio content — songs, podcasts, or audio-books. If you don't have any audio on your iPhone yet, we humbly suggest that you get some (flip back to Chapter 3 and follow the instructions) before you read the rest of this chapter — or the next chapter for that matter.

©iStockphoto.com/Michael Beck

Okay, now that you have some audio content on your iPhone to play with, are you ready to rock?

Introducing the iPod inside Your iPhone

To use your iPhone as an iPod, just tap the iPod icon in the bottom-right corner of the Home screen. At the bottom of the screen that appears, you should see five icons: Playlists, Artists, Songs, Video, and More.

If you don't see these icons, tap the Back button in the top-left corner of the screen (the one that looks like a little arrow pointing to the left).

Or, if you're holding your iPhone sideways (the long edges parallel to the ground), rotate it 90 degrees so it's upright (the short edges parallel to the ground).

You'll understand why your iPhone's orientation matters when you read the section on Cover Flow, which is coming up in a few pages.

Playing with playlists

Tap the Playlists icon at the bottom of the screen and a list of playlists appears. If you don't have any playlists on your iPhone, don't sweat. Just know that if you had some, this is where they'd be. (Playlists let you organize songs around a particular theme or mood: opera arias, romantic ballads, British invasion, whatever.)

Tap a playlist and you see a list of the songs it contains. If the list is longer than one screen, flick upwards to scroll down. Tap a song in the list and it plays.

And that's all there is to selecting and playing a song from a playlist.

Artistic license

Now let's find and play a song by the artist's name instead of by playlist. Tap the Artists icon at the bottom of the screen and a list of artists appears.

Tap an artist's name and a list of songs by that artist appears. If the list is longer than one screen, flick upwards to scroll down. Tap a song in this list and it plays.

Are you starting to see a pattern here?

Song selection

Finally, let's find a song by its title and play it. Tap the Songs icon at the bottom of the screen and a list of songs appears.

Now chances are your list of songs is quite a bit longer than your lists of playlists and artists. So in addition to flicking upwards to scroll down, you can tap a letter on the right side of the screen to jump to songs that start with that letter. In Figure 7-1, for example, that letter is *T*.

Figure 7-1: Tap the *T* on the right side of the screen to jump to song titles that begin with *T*.

Taking Control of Your Tunes

Now that you have the basics down, let's look at some of the other things you can do when your iPhone is in its iPod mode.

Go with the (cover) flow

Finding tracks by playlist, artist, or song is cool, but finding them with Cover Flow is even cooler. Cover Flow lets you browse your music collection by its album artwork. To use Cover Flow, turn your iPhone sideways (that is, long edges parallel to the ground). As long as you're not browsing or viewing video (and, of course, you've tapped the iPod icon on the Home screen so your iPhone behaves like an iPod), Cover Flow fills the screen, as shown in Figure 7-2.

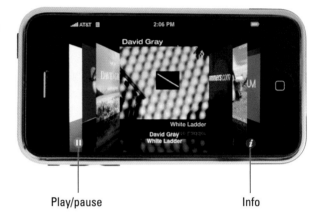

Play/pause   Info

Figure 7-2: Go with the Cover Flow.

It's simple to scan your cover art in Cover Flow. All you have to do is drag or flick your finger left or right on the screen and the covers go flying by. Flick or drag quickly and the covers whiz by; flick or drag slowly and the covers move leisurely. Or tap a particular cover on the left or right of the current (centered) cover and that cover jumps to the center.

Try it, you'll like it! Now here's how to put Cover Flow to work for you:

- ✔ To see the tracks (songs) on an album, tap the cover when it's centered or tap the info button (the little *i*) in the lower-right corner of the screen. The track list appears.

- ✔ To play a track, tap its name in the list. If the list is long, scroll by dragging or flicking up and down on it.

- ✔ To go back to Cover Flow, tap the title bar at the top of the track list or tap the little *i* button again.

- ✔ To play or pause the current song, tap the play/pause button in the lower-left corner.

If no cover art exists for an album in your collection, the iPhone displays a plain-looking cover decorated with musical notes. The name of the album appears below this generic cover.

And that, friends, is all there is to the iPhone's cool Cover Flow mode.

Flow's not here right now

As you saw earlier in the chapter, when you hold your iPhone vertically (the short edges parallel to the ground) and tap the Playlists, Artists, or Songs button, you see a list instead of Cover Flow.

The controls are different depending on which way you hold your iPhone as well. When you hold your iPhone vertically, as shown in Figure 7-3, you see controls that don't appear when you hold your iPhone sideways. And furthermore,

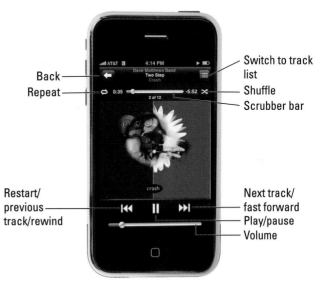

Back

Repeat

Switch to track list

Shuffle

Scrubber bar

Restart/ previous track/rewind

Next track/ fast forward

Play/pause

Volume

Figure 7-3: Hold your iPhone vertically when you play a track and these are the controls you'll see.

the controls you see when viewing the Playlists, Artists, or Songs lists are slightly different than the controls you see when a song is playing.

Here's how to use the controls that appear when the iPhone is vertical :

- ✔ **Back button:** Tap this to return to whichever list you used last — Playlists, Artists, or Songs.

- ✔ **Switch to track list button:** Tap this to switch to a list of tracks.

   If you don't see the next three controls — the repeat button, the scrubber, and the shuffle button — tap the album cover once to make them appear.

- ✔ **Repeat button:** Tap once to repeat songs in the current album or list. The button turns blue. Tap it again to repeat the current song over and over again; the blue button displays the number 1 when it's in this mode. Tap it again to turn it off. The button goes back to its original color, gray.

✓ **Scrubber bar:** Drag the little dot (the playhead) along the scrubber bar to skip to any point within the song.

✓ **Shuffle button:** Tap once to shuffle songs and play them in random order. The button turns blue when shuffling is enabled. Tap it again to play songs in order again. The button goes back to its original color, gray.

You can also shuffle tracks in any list of songs — such as playlists or albums — by tapping the word *Shuffle,* which appears at the top of the list. Regardless of whether the shuffle button has been tapped, this technique always plays songs in that list in random order.

✓ **Restart/previous track/rewind button:** Tap this once to go to the beginning of the track. Tap it twice to go to the start of the previous track in the list. Touch and hold it to rewind through the song at double speed.

✓ **Play/pause button:** Tap this to play or pause the song.

✓ **Next track/fast-forward button:** Tap this to skip to the next track in the list. Touch and hold it to fast forward through the song at double speed.

✓ **Volume control:** Drag the little dot left or right to reduce or increase the volume level.

If you're using the headset included with your iPhone, you can squeeze the mic to pause, and squeeze it again to play. You can also squeeze it twice in rapid succession to skip to the next song. Sweet!

When you tap the switch to track list button, the iPhone screen and the controls change, as shown in Figure 7-4. And here's how to use *those* controls:

✓ **Switch to now playing button:** Tap this to switch to the Now Playing screen for the current track (refer to Figure 7-3).

✓ **Rating bar:** Drag across the rating bar to rate the current track with zero to five stars. The track shown in Figure 7-4 has a four-star rating.

Figure 7-4: Tap the switch to track list button and these new controls appear.

The tracks are the songs in the current list (album, playlist, artist, and so on) and the current track indicator shows you which song is currently playing (or paused). Tap any song in a track list to play it.

And that, friends, is pretty much all you need to know to enjoy listening to music (and podcasts and audiobooks, too) on your iPhone.

Customizing Your Audio Experience

We should cover a few more things before you move on to the video side of your iPhone-as-an-iPod in Chapter 8. In this section you find a bunch of stuff you can do to make your listening experience even better.

If you still want more . . .

If you'd prefer to browse through your audio collection by criteria other than playlists, artists, or songs, there is a way. That way is to tap the More button at the bottom-right corner of the screen. The More list appears. Tap a choice in the list — albums, audiobooks, compilations, composers, genres, or podcasts — and your audio collection is organized by your criterion.

But wait, there's more. You can swap out the Playlists, Artists, Songs, and Video buttons for ones that better suit your needs. So, for example, if you listen to a lot of podcasts and never watch video, you can replace the Video button with a Podcasts button.

Here's how:

1. **Tap the More button at the bottom-right corner of the screen.**
2. **Tap the Edit button at the top-left corner of the screen.**
3. **Drag any button on the screen — Albums, Podcasts, Audiobooks, Genres, Composers, Compilations — onto the button at the bottom of the screen that you want it to replace.**
4. **You can also rearrange the five buttons now by dragging them to the left or right.**
5. **When everything is just the way you like it, tap the Done button to return to the More list.**

You can always browse your audio collection by buttons you replace this way by tapping the More button and choosing the item that corresponds to the button you replaced in the More list.

Setting preferences

You can change a few preference settings to customize your iPhone-as-an-iPod experience.

Play all songs at the same volume level

iTunes has an option called Sound Check that automatically adjusts the level of songs so they play at the same volume relative to each other. That way, one song never blasts out your ears even if the recording is much louder than the song before or after it. To tell the iPhone to use these volume settings, you first have to turn on the feature in iTunes on your computer. Here's how to do that:

1. **Choose iTunes⇨Preferences (Mac) or Edit⇨Preferences (PC).**
2. **Click the Playback tab.**
3. **Select the Sound Check check box to enable it.**

Now you need to tell the iPhone to use the Sound Check settings from iTunes. Here's how to do *that*:

1. **Tap the Settings icon on the iPhone's Home screen.**
2. **Tap iPod in the list of settings.**
3. **Tap Sound Check to turn it on.**

Set the audiobook playing speed

You can make audiobooks play a bit faster or slower than usual if you like. To do so:

1. **Tap the Settings icon on the Home screen.**
2. **Tap iPod in the list of settings.**
3. **Tap Audiobook in the list of iPod settings.**
4. **Tap Slower of Faster to slow down or speed up audiobook playback.**

Choose an equalizer setting

An equalizer increases or decreases the relative levels of specific frequencies to enhance the sound you hear. Some equalizer settings emphasize the bass notes (low end) in a song; other equalizer settings make the higher frequencies more apparent. The iPhone has more than a dozen equalizer presets, with names such as Acoustic, Bass Booster, Bass Reducer, Dance, Electronic, Pop, and Rock. Each one is ostensibly tailored to a specific type of music.

The way to find out whether you prefer using equalization is to listen to music while trying out different settings. To do that, first start listening to a song you like. Then, while the song is playing:

1. **Tap the Home button on the front of your iPhone.**

2. **Tap the Settings icon on the Home screen.**

3. **Tap iPod in the list of settings.**

4. **Tap EQ in the list of iPod settings.**

5. **Tap different EQ presets (Pop, Rock, R&B, Dance, and so on) and listen carefully to the way it changes how the song sounds.**

6. **When you find an equalizer preset you think sounds good, tap the Home button and you're finished.**

If you don't like any of the presets, tap Off at the top of the EQ list to turn off the equalizer.

If you've set an equalizer preset for a song using the Track Info window in iTunes, that setting is applied automatically to the song when you sync it to your iPhone. That's pretty cool.

Set a volume limit for music (and videos)

You can instruct your iPhone to limit the loudest listening level for audio or video. To do so:

1. **Tap the Settings icon on the Home screen.**

2. **Tap iPod in the list of settings.**

3. **Tap Volume Limit in the list of iPod settings.**

4. **Drag the slider to adjust the maximum volume level to your liking.**

5. **(Optional) Tap Lock Volume Limit to assign a four-digit passcode to this setting so others can't easily change it.**

The Volume Limit setting only limits the volume of music and videos. It doesn't apply to podcasts or audiobooks. And although it does work with any headset, headphones, or speakers plugged into the headset jack on your iPhone, it does not affect sound played through your iPhone's internal speaker.

Make a playlist on your iPhone

Of course you can make playlists in iTunes and sync them with your iPhone, but you can also create playlists on your iPhone when you're out and about. Here's how:

1. **Tap the iPod icon in the bottom-right corner of the Home screen.**

2. **Tap the Playlists button at the bottom of the screen.**

3. **Tap the first item in the list, On-the-Go.**

   An alphabetical list of all the songs on your iPhone appears. To the right of each song is a little plus sign.

4. **Tap the plus sign next to a song name to add the song to your On-the-Go playlist.**

   To add all of these songs to your On-the-Go playlist, tap the plus sign next to the first item in the list, Add All Songs.

5. **Tap the Done button in the top-right corner.**

If you create an On-the-Go playlist and then sync your iPhone with your computer, that playlist will be saved both on the iPhone and in iTunes on your computer. The first time you save one it will be named On-the-Go 1 automatically. Subsequent lists you create will be auto-named On-the-Go 2, On-the-Go 3, and so on.

The playlists remain until you delete them from iTunes. To do that, select the playlist's name in the source list and then press Delete or Backspace.

You can also edit your On-the-Go playlist. To do so, first tap the Playlists button at the bottom of the screen, tap the first item in the list, On-the-Go, and tap the Edit button. Then:

✔ **To move a song up or down in the On-the-Go playlist:** A little icon with three gray bars appears to the right of each song. Drag the icon up to move the song higher in the list or down to move the song lower in the list.

✔ **To add more songs to the On-the-Go playlist:** Tap the plus button in the top-left corner.

✔ **To delete a song from the On-the-Go playlist:** Tap the minus sign to the left of the song name. Note that deleting a song from the On-the-Go playlist doesn't remove the song from your iPhone.

✔ **To clear the On-the-Go playlist of all songs:** Tap the first item in the list, Clear Playlist.

When you've finished editing, tap the Done button in the top-right corner.

And that's all there is to creating and managing On-the-Go playlists.

Set a sleep timer

If you like to fall asleep with music playing but don't want to leave your iPhone playing music all night long, you can turn on its sleep timer.

Here's how:

1. **Tap the Clock button on the Home screen.**
2. **Tap the Timer icon in the lower-right corner.**
3. **Set the number of hours and minutes you want the iPhone to play, and then tap the When Timer Ends button.**
4. **Tap the first item in the list, Sleep iPod.**
5. **Tap the Set button in the top-right corner.**
6. **Tap the big green Start button.**

That's it! After the appropriate period of time your iPod will stop playing and your iPhone will go to sleep.

iPhone Video: Seeing Is Believing

*P*icture this scene: The smell of popcorn permeates the room as you and your family congregate to watch the latest Hollywood blockbuster. A motion picture soundtrack swells up. The images on the screen are stunning. And all eyes are fixed on the iPhone.

Okay, here comes the reality check. The iPhone is not going to replace a wall-sized high-definition television as the centerpiece of your home theater. But we do want to emphasize that with its glorious widescreen 3½-inch display — the best we've seen on a handheld device — watching movies and other videos on the iPhone can be a cinematic delight.

Let's get on with the show!

Finding Stuff to Watch

The video you'll watch on the iPhone generally falls into one of four categories:

©iStockphoto.com/Skip O'donnell

✔ **Movies, TV shows, and music videos that reside in iTunes software on your PC or Mac that you synchronize with your iPhone.** (For more on synchronization, refer to Chapter 3.) You can watch these by tapping the iPod icon at the bottom of the Home screen and then tapping Videos.

Apple's own iTunes Store features dedicated sections for purchasing episodes of TV shows (from *The Larry Sanders Show* to *Teletubbies*) and movies (such as *Finding Nemo* or *The Queen*). Typical price as of this writing are $1.99 per episode for TV shows and $9.99 for feature films.

✐ **The boatload of video podcasts, just about all of them free, featured in the iTunes Store.** Podcasts started out as another form of Internet radio, though instead of listening to live streams you downloaded files onto your computer to take in at your leisure. There are still lots of audio podcasts, but the focus here is on video.

✐ **Homegrown videos from the popular YouTube Internet site.** Apple obviously thinks highly of YouTube because it devoted a dedicated Home screen icon to the site. More on YouTube's special place in the iPhone later in this chapter.

✐ **The movies you've created in iMovie software on the Mac or other programs on the PC.** Plus all the other videos you may have downloaded from the Internet.

Are we compatible?

Sidebars in this book are considered optional reading, but we secretly hope you'll digest every word because you may discover something or be entertained or both. But you can safely skip the material contained herein, no matter how much you want to curry favor with your teachers, um, authors.

Still, we present this list of video formats supported by the iPhone as a courtesy to those with geek aspirations (you know who you are). And just to point out how absurd the world of tech can sound sometimes — even from a consumer-friendly company such as Apple — we are lifting this passage from Apple's Web site verbatim:

Video formats supported: H.264 video, up to 1.5 Mbps, 640 by 480 pixels, 30 frames per second, Low-Complexity version of the H.264 Baseline Profile with AAC-LC audio up to 160 Kbps, 48kHz, stereo audio in .m4v, .mp4, and .mov file formats;

H.264 video, up to 768 Kbps, 320 by 240 pixels, 30 frames per second, Baseline Profile up to Level 1.3 with AAC-LC audio up to 160 Kbps, 48kHz, stereo audio in .m4v, .mp4, and .mov file formats; MPEG-4 video, up to 2.5 Mbps, 640 by 480 pixels, 30 frames per second, Simple Profile with AAC-LC audio up to 160 Kbps, 48kHz, stereo audio in .m4v, .mp4, and .mov file formats

Got all that? Here's the takeaway message: The iPhone works with a whole bunch of video, though not everything you'll want to watch will make it through. And you may not know if it will play until you try. Indeed, several Internet video standards, notably Adobe Flash, Java, Real, and Windows Media Video, were not supported when this book was in production. (This may have changed by the time you read this.) However, if something doesn't play now it may well in the future because Apple has the ability to upgrade the iPhone through software.

You may have to prepare these videos so that they'll play on your iPhone. To do so, highlight the video in question after it resides in your iTunes library. Go to the Advanced menu in iTunes, and click Convert Selection for iPod.

For more on compatibility, check out the "Are we compatible?" sidebar (but read it at your own risk).

Playing Video

Now that you know what you want to watch, here's how to watch it:

1. **On the Home screen, tap the iPod icon and then tap the Videos icon.**

   Your list of videos pops up. As shown in Figure 8-1, videos are segregated by category (Movies, TV Shows, Music Videos, Podcasts) and accompanied by thumbnail images and the length of the video.

2. **Flick your finger to scroll through the list, and then tap the video you want to play. You'll see a spinning circle for just a moment and then the video will begin.**

3. **Turn the device to its side because the iPhone plays video only in landscape, or widescreen, mode.**

   For movies, this is a great thing. You can watch flicks as the filmmaker intended, in a cinematic *aspect ratio*.

4. **Now that the video is playing, tap the screen to display the controls shown in Figure 8-2.**

5. **Tap the controls that follow as needed:**

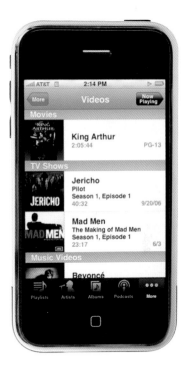

Figure 8-1: Choosing the video to watch.

   - To play or pause the video, tap the play/pause button.

   - Drag the volume slider to the right to raise the volume and to the left to lower it. Alternatively, use the physical Volume buttons to control the audio levels. If the video is oriented properly, the buttons will be to the bottom left of the iPhone.

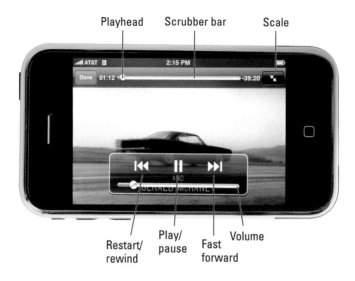

Figure 8-2: Controlling the video.

- Tap the restart/rewind button to restart the video or tap and hold the same button to rewind.

- Tap and hold the fast-forward button to advance the video. You can skip ahead also by dragging the playhead along the scrubber bar.

- Tap the scale button to toggle between filling the entire screen with video or fitting the video to the screen. Alternatively, you can double-tap the video to go back and forth between fitting and filling the screen.

  Here's the distinction between fitting and filling. Fitting the video to the screen displays the film in its theatrical aspect ratio. But you may see black bars above or below the video (or to its sides), which some people don't like. On the other hand, filling the entire screen with the video may crop or trim the sides or top of the picture, so you aren't seeing the complete scene that the director shot.

6. **Tap the screen again to make the controls go away (or just wait for them to go away on their own).**

7. **Tap Done when you've finished watching (you'll have to summon the controls back if they're not already present).**

   You return to the iPhone's video menu screen.

If you make it to the end of a movie or other video — so did the butler do it, or what? — the iPhone generously offers to delete the film to free up space, as shown in Figure 8-3. Tap Keep or Delete depending on your preference. If you tap Delete, the iPhone will ask whether you're sure. Don't sweat it. If you ever change your mind, just sync the movie again from iTunes.

Figure 8-3: Making room for the next flick.

To manually delete a video, swipe left or right over the video listing. Then tap the small red Delete button that materializes. To confirm your intention, tap the larger Delete button that appears.

Sometimes you want to hear a song from a music video but don't want to watch it. Instead of tapping the Videos icon to grab that selection, choose the ditty by tapping the Songs or Artists icon instead.

Hey You, It's YouTube

YouTube has come to define video sharing on the Internet. The wildly popular site, now owned by Google, has become so powerful that American presidential hopefuls and even politicians in other countries campaign and hold debates there. As you might imagine, YouTube has also generated controversy. The site has been banned in some foreign countries. And Viacom sued YouTube for more than $1 billion over alleged copyright infringements. (We'll leave that fight to the lawyers.)

All the while, of course, YouTube staked a humongous claim on mainstream culture. That's because YouTube is, well, about you and us and our pets and so on. It is the cyberdestination, as YouTube boldly proclaims, to "Broadcast Yourself."

Apple has afforded YouTube its own cherished icon on the Home screen. The company announced that more than 10,000 YouTube streaming videos were available on the iPhone at the time of its end-of-June 2007 launch, with the full catalog promised by the fall of 2007.

Why the delay? The back catalog of YouTube videos are being converted to the *H.264* video compression standard that the iPhone (and another Apple product called Apple TV) can recognize.

As with other videos, you can tap the screen when a YouTube video plays to bring up hidden video controls. Many of these controls are identical to the controls in Figure 8-2. But as Figure 8-4 shows, YouTube displays special controls of its own, notably for adding bookmarks and sending e-mail links of the video you're watching.

Bookmark   E-mail

Figure 8-4: YouTube video controls.

Hunting for YouTube gems

So where exactly do YouTubers find the videos that will offer them a blissful, albeit brief, respite from the rest of their day? By tapping on any of the following:

- **Featured:** Videos recommended by YouTube's own staffers.
- **Most Viewed:** What the YouTube community is watching. Tap All to see the most watched YouTube videos of all time. Tap Today or This Week to check out the videos most currently in vogue.

✒ **Bookmarks:** After stumbling on a video you like, bookmark it by tapping the Bookmark control.

✒ **Search:** Tap the Search icon, and then tap the blank YouTube search field at the top of the screen. Up pops one of the iPhone's virtual keyboards. Type a search phrase and then tap the Search button to generate results. (In Figure 8-5, we typed Steve Jobs.)

✒ **More:** Tapping More leads to more buttons or icons. As in those that follow . . .

✒ **Most Recent:** Newly submitted videos.

✒ **Top Rated:** The people's choice. YouTube's audience chooses the best.

✒ **History:** Videos you recently viewed.

Figure 8-5: Finding Steve Jobs on YouTube.

Only four YouTube icons (besides the More button) appear at the bottom of the screen at any one time. But say you are more likely to tap the Top Rated icon rather than the Bookmarks icon to get to videos you want to check out. Rather than having to tap More each time you want to tap Top Rated, you can make it one of your Fab Four icons.

To change the icons shown on that first YouTube screen, tap More and then tap Edit. Then simply drag your preferred icon (Top Rated in this example) over the one you want to relegate to the YouTube bench (Bookmarks in this case). You can also rearrange the order of the icons by dragging them left or right.

While the movie you've selected is downloading — and how fast it arrives depends on your network coverage from AT&T or Wi-Fi, as discussed in greater detail in Chapter 10 — you see a black-and-grey screen with video controls and the YouTube logo. This screen is shown in Figure 8-6. The controls disappear once the movie starts playing.

Figure 8-6: Waiting to be entertained.

Sharing YouTube videos

We were as enthralled as that harshest of critics Simon Cowell was by Paul Potts, the British mobile phone worker turned opera singer. His star turn on the *American Idol*-like *Britain's Got Talent* has been immortalized on YouTube by millions.

You can share such a video as you are watching it, by tapping the e-mail button (refer to Figure 8-4). When you do so, one of the iPhone's virtual keyboards pops up. iPhone has already filled in the e-mail subject line with the name of the video. And the body of the message is populated with a link to the video on YouTube. All you need to do is fill in the To field with the e-mail address of the person you are sending the link to along with any additional comments.

Alternatively, from the list of videos, tap the blue button with the right-pointing arrow to see all sorts of details on a particular video. You'll see a description of the video, the number of people who viewed it, the date it was added, and other information. From there, tap the Share button to bring up the e-mail program described in the preceding paragraph.

With that, let's roll the closing credits to this chapter.

9

You Oughta Be in Pictures

amera phones may outsell dedicated digital cameras nowadays, but with relatively few exceptions, they're rather mediocre picture takers. Come to think of it, most mobile phones don't show off digital images all that well either.

Of course, most mobile phones aren't iPhones.

The device you have recently purchased (or are lusting after) is a pretty spectacular photo viewer. And though its built-in digital camera isn't the one we'd rely on for snapping pictures during an African safari, say, or even Junior's fast-paced soccer game, the iPhone in your steady hands can produce perfectly acceptable photos.

Over the next few pages, you discover how best to exploit the iPhone's camera. We then move on to the real magic — making the digital photos that reside on the iPhone come alive — whether you imported them from your computer or captured them with the iPhone's camera.

©iStockphoto.com/Vasko Miokovic

Taking Your Best Shot

Like many applications on the iPhone, you'll find the Camera application icon on the Home screen. It's positioned on the upper row of icons all the way to the right and adjacent to its next-of-kin, the Photos icon. We'll be tapping both icons throughout this chapter.

Let's snap an image now:

1. **Tap the Camera icon on the Home screen to turn the iPhone into the rough equivalent of a Kodak Instamatic, minus the film and flash, of course.**

2. **Keep your eyes fixed on the iPhone's display.**

   The first thing you'll notice on the screen is something resembling a closed camera shutter. But that shutter will open in about a second, revealing a window into what the camera lens sees. In case you were wondering, the lens is hiding behind the small foxhole at the top-left corner of the back of the iPhone. (The position of the camera lens is shown in Chapter 1, Figure 1-3.)

3. **Aim the camera at whatever you want to shoot, using the iPhone's brilliant 3½-inch display as your viewfinder.**

   We've been marveling at the display throughout this book; the camera application gives us another reason to do so.

4. **When you are satisfied with what's in the frame, tap the camera icon at the bottom of the screen (see Figure 9-1) to snap the picture.**

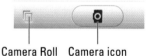

Camera Roll   Camera icon
icon

Figure 9-1: Say cheese.

   You'll experience momentary shutter lag, so be sure to remain still. When the shutter reopens, you'll see the image you have just shot, but just for a blink. The screen will again function as a viewfinder so you can capture your next image.

   And that's it, you've snapped your very first iPhone picture.

5. **Repeat Steps 3 and 4 to capture additional images.**

If you position the iPhone sideways while snapping an image, the picture is saved in landscape mode.

Tasty pixels and other digital camera treats

The iPhone is a 2-megapixel digital camera. And if you've been shopping for a digital camera of any type, you are already aware that megapixels are marketed like chocolate chips. You know, the more of them, the tastier the cookie, or in the case of digital photography, the better the camera. But that may not always be true. The number of megapixels counts for sure, but so do a bevy of other factors, including lens quality and shutter lag.

The important thing to remember about megapixels is that they are a measure of a camera's resolution, or picture sharpness, which becomes particularly important to folks who want to blow up prints well beyond snapshot size. For example, you'd probably want at least a 4-megapixel standalone digital camera if you hope to print decent 8-by-10-inch or larger photos.

Which brings us back to the iPhone. From a camera phone perspective, 2 megapixels is still considered fairly decent, though you can certainly find more and more cell phones with a higher megapixel count. Still, we figure most of you will be more than satisfied with the pictures you take with the iPhone, so long as you keep your expectations in check and don't expect to produce poster-size images.

We're obliged to point out, however, that the digital camera in the initial iPhone lacks some features found on rival camera phones, notably a flash and the ability to shoot short video clips. There are no advanced editing features either.

All that said, those other camera phones can't hold a candle to the iPhone when it comes to showing off those images, as the rest of this chapter proves. The iPhone's high-resolution 480-x-320 screen — yep, it's measured in pixels — is simply stunning.

There are a couple more things to keep in mind while snapping pictures with the iPhone.

In our experience, the iPhone camera button is super sensitive. We have accidentally taken a few rotten snapshots because of it. So be careful; a gentle tap is all that's required to snap an image.

Moreover, we're not sure Apple had this in mind, but the dock that was supplied with the iPhone doubles as a handy mini-tripod (albeit without three legs to stand on). It's hardly a perfect solution, but you can leave the iPhone docked and take a picture, without worrying too much about keeping the camera steady.

Importing Pictures

You needn't use only the iPhone's digital camera to get pictures onto the device, of course, and in most cases, we suspect that you won't. Instead, you can synchronize photos from a PC or Macintosh using the iTunes Summary pane, which is described in Chapter 3. (The assumption here is that you already know how to get pictures onto your computer.)

Quickie reminder: On a Mac you can sync photos via iPhoto software version 4.03 or later and Aperture. And on a PC, you can sync with Adobe Photoshop Album 2.0 or later and Adobe Photoshop Elements 3.0 or later. Alternatively, with both computers, you can sync with any folder containing pictures.

When iPhoto is connected to your computer, click the Photos tab in the Summary pane. Then click the appropriate check boxes to specify the pictures and photos you want to synchronize. Or choose All Photos and Albums, if you have enough storage on the iPhone to accommodate them.

Syncing pictures is a two-way process, so photos captured with the iPhone's digital camera can also end up in the photo library on your computer.

Where Have All My Pictures Gone?

So where exactly do your pictures hang out on the iPhone? The ones you snapped on iPhone end up in a photo album appropriately dubbed the Camera Roll. Of course, the photos you imported are readily available too (and grouped in the same albums they were on the computer). We'll show you not only where they are, but how to display them and share them with others — and how to dispose of the duds that don't measure up to your lofty photographic standards.

So get ready to literally get your fingers on the pix (without having to worry about smudging them):

1. **From the Camera application, tap the Camera Roll icon (refer to Figure 9-1). Or you can tap the Photos icon on the Home screen, and then tap Camera Roll or any other album in the list of Photo Albums.**

   The shutter closes for just an instant and is replaced by the screen depicted in Figure 9-2, which shows thumbnail images of the complete roll of pictures you've shot with the iPhone. This is the Camera Roll.

Using the first method, you can access only the Camera Roll. Using the second method, you can access the Camera Roll and all your other photo albums.

2. **Browse through the thumbnail images in the album until you find the picture you want to display.**

   If the thumbnail you have in mind doesn't appear on this screen, flick your finger up or down to scroll through the pictures rapidly or use a slower dragging motion to pore through the images more deliberately.

3. **Tap the appropriate thumbnail.**

   The picture you've selected fills the entire screen.

4. **Tap the screen again.**

   The picture controls appear, as shown in Figure 9-3. We discuss what these do later.

5. **To make the controls disappear, tap the screen again, or just wait a few seconds and they'll go away on their own.**

Figure 9-2: Your pictures at a glance.

6. **To transform the iPhone back into a picture-taker rather than a picture-viewer, make sure the picture controls are displayed and then tap the camera icon at the upper-right.**

   Note that this option is available only if you arrived at the Camera Roll from the Camera application. If you didn't, you have to back out of this application altogether and tap the Home button and then the Camera application icon to call the iPhone's digital camera back into duty.

7. **To return to the thumbnails view of your Camera Roll or the thumbnails for any of your other albums, make sure the picture controls are displayed. Then tap the Camera Roll button at the upper left.**

   The Camera Roll button will carry the name of one of your other photo albums if you are trying to return to that collection of pictures instead.

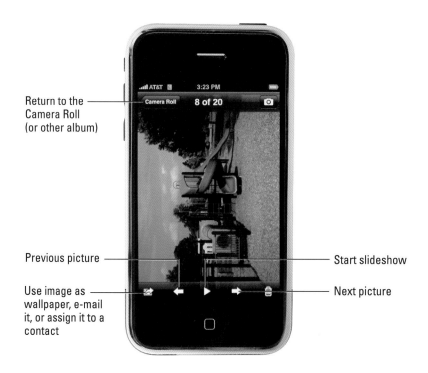

Return to the Camera Roll (or other album)

Previous picture

Use image as wallpaper, e-mail it, or assign it to a contact

Start slideshow

Next picture

Figure 9-3: Picture controls.

Admiring Pictures

Photographs are meant to be seen, of course, not buried in the digital equivalent of a shoebox. And the iPhone affords you some neat ways to manipulate, view, and share your best photos.

We already know from the preceding section how to find a photo and view it full-screen and bring up picture controls. But you can do a lot of maneuvering of pictures without summoning those controls. Here are some options:

- ✐ **Skipping ahead or viewing the previous picture:** Flick your finger left or right or tap the left or right arrow controls.

- ✐ **Landscape or portrait:** The iPhone's wizardry (or more specifically, the device's accelerometer sensor) is at work. When you turn the iPhone sideways, the picture automatically reorients itself from portrait to landscape mode, as the images in Figure 9-4 show. Pictures shot in landscape mode fill the screen when you rotate the iPhone. Rotate the device back to portrait mode, and the picture readjusts accordingly.

✓ **Zoom:** Double-tap to zoom in on an image and make it larger. Do so again to zoom out and make it smaller. Alternatively, take your thumb and index finger and pinch to zoom in, or un-pinch the photo to zoom out.

✓ **Pan and scroll:** This cool little feature is practically guaranteed to make you the life of the party. Once you've zoomed in on a picture, drag it around the screen with your finger. Besides impressing your friends, you can bring the part of the image you most care about front and center. That'll let you zoom in on Fido's adorable face as opposed to, say, the unflattering picture of the person holding the dog in his or her lap.

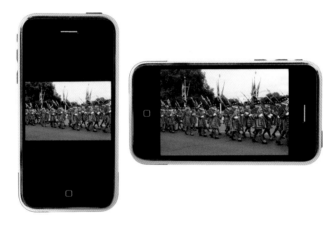

Figure 9-4: The same picture in portrait and landscape modes.

Launching Slideshows

Those of us who store a lot of photographs on computers are familiar with running slideshows of those images. It's a breeze to replicate the experience on the iPhone:

1. **Choose your Camera Roll or another album from the Photo Albums list.**

   To do so, tap the Photos icon from the Home screen or tap the Camera Roll button in the Camera application.

2. **If you see the play button at the bottom of the thumbnails screen, tap it and you're finished.**

3. **If you don't see the play button at the bottom of the thumbnails screen, tap a thumbnail to choose a photo, and then tap the play button.**

   You may have to tap the picture a second time to bring up the play button.

Enjoy the show.

Special slideshow effects

You can alter the length of time each slide is shown, change the transition effects between pictures, and display images in random order. Here's how.

From the Home screen, tap Settings and then scroll down and tap Photos. Then tap any of the following to make changes:

- **Play Each Slide For:** You have five choices (2 seconds, 3 seconds, 5 seconds, 10 seconds, 20 seconds). Tap the Photos button when you are finished to return to the main Settings screen for Photos.

- **Transition:** This is the effect you see when you move from one slide to the next. Again, there are five choices (cube, dissolve, ripple, wipe across, wipe down). Why not try them all to see what you like? Tap the Photos button when you are finished.

- **Repeat:** If turned on, the slideshow continues to loop until you stop it. If off, the slideshow for your Camera Roll or album plays just once. The Repeat control may be counterintuitive for some. If Off is showing, tap it to turn on the Repeat function. If On is showing, tap it to turn off the Repeat function.

- **Shuffle:** Turning this feature on plays slides in random order. As with the Repeat feature, tap Off to turn on shuffle or tap On to turn off random playback.

Tap the Home button to leave Settings and return to the Home screen.

Adding music to your slideshow

Ed loves backing up slideshows with Sinatra, Sarah Vaughan, or Sarah McLachlan, among numerous other artists. Bob loves using Beatles songs or stately classical music.

Adding music to a slideshow couldn't be easier. Just tap iPod and begin playing a song. Then return to the Photo application to start up a slideshow as described in the beginning of the "Launching Slideshows" section.

Deleting pictures

We told a tiny fib by intimating that photographs are meant to be seen. We should have amended that by saying that *some* pictures are meant to be seen. For others, you can't get rid of them fast enough. Fortunately, the iPhone makes it a cinch to bury the evidence:

1. **From the appropriate photo album, tap the objectionable photograph.**

2. **Tap to display the picture controls, provided they're not already displayed.**

3. **Tap the trash can icon.**

4. **Tap Delete (or Cancel if you change your mind).**

   The photo gets sucked into the trash can and mercifully disappears.

More (Not So) Stupid Picture Tricks

You can take advantage of the photos on the iPhone in three more ways. In each case you tap the picture and make sure the picture controls are displayed. Then tap the icon at the bottom left — the one that looks like an arrow trying to escape from a rectangle. That displays the trio of choices shown in Figure 9-5. Let's explore these now.

Figure 9-5: Look at what else I can do!

- **Use as Wallpaper:** The default background image on the iPhone when you unlock the device is a gorgeous view of Earth. Dramatic though it may be, you probably have an even better photograph to use as the iPhone's wallpaper. A picture of your spouse, your kids, or your pets, perhaps?

  When you tap the Use as Wallpaper button, you see what the present image will look like as the iPhone's background picture. And as Figure 9-6 shows, you are given the opportunity to move the picture around and resize it, through the now familiar action of dragging or pinching against the screen with your fingers. When you're satisfied with what the wallpaper will look like, tap the Set Wallpaper button. Per usual, you also have the option to tap Cancel. More on Wallpaper in Chapter 13.

- **Email Photo:** Some photos are so precious that you just have to share them with family members and friends. When you tap Email Photo, the picture is automatically embedded in the body of an outgoing e-mail message. Use the virtual keyboard to enter the e-mail addresses, subject line, and any additional comments you'd like to add. You know, something profound like, "Isn't this a great looking photo?" (Skip to Chapter 11 for more info on using e-mail.)

- **Assign to Contact:** If you assign a picture to someone in your Contacts list, this image will pop up when you receive a call from the person. To make it happen, tap Assign to Contact. Your list of contacts appears on the screen. Scroll up or down the list to find the person who matches the picture of the moment. As with the wallpaper example, you can drag and resize the picture to get it just right. Then tap Set Photo.

As you may recall from Chapter 4, you can also assign a photo to a contact by starting out in Contacts. As a refresher, start by tapping Phone, and then tapping Contacts. From Contacts, choose the person, tap Edit, and then tap Add

Figure 9-6: Beautifying the iPhone with wallpaper.

Photo. At that point, you can take a new picture with the iPhone's digital camera or select an existing portrait from one of your onboard picture albums.

To change the picture you've assigned to a person, tap his or her name in the Contacts list, tap Edit, and then tap the person's thumbnail picture, which also carries the label Edit. From there, you can take another photo with the iPhone's digital camera, select another photo from one of your albums, edit the photo you are already using (by resizing and dragging it to a new position), or delete the photo.

You have just passed Photography 101 on the iPhone. We trust the coursework was a, forgive the pun, snap.

Part IV
The Internet iPhone

The commercials for the iPhone say it provides you with the real Internet — and it does. So in this part we look at the Internet components of your phone, starting with a chapter covering the best Web browser ever to grace a handheld device, Safari. We see how to take advantage of links and bookmarks and how to open multiple Web pages at the same time. We show you how to run a Web search on an iPhone. And we spend time discussing EDGE and Wi-Fi too, the wireless networks that are compatible with the device.

Then we visit the Mail program and see how easy it is to set up e-mail accounts and to send and receive real honest-to-goodness e-mail messages and attachments.

Finally, we examine three superb Web-enabled applications. In Maps, you determine the businesses and restaurants you'd like to visit, and get driving directions and the traffic en route. In Weather, you get the forecast for all the cities you live in or plan on visiting. And in Stocks, you can get the lowdown on how well the equities in your portfolio are performing.

10

Going On a Mobile Safari

"The Internet in your pocket."

That's what Apple promised the iPhone would bring to the public when the product was announced in January 2007. Steve Jobs & Co. have come tantalizingly close to delivering on that pledge.

For years, the cell phone industry has been offering some sort of watered-down mobile version of the Internet, but the approaches fall far short of what you've come to experience sitting in front of a computer.

Apple, however, has managed to replicate the real-deal Internet with the iPhone. Web pages look like Web pages do on a Windows PC or Macintosh, right down to swanky graphics and pictures — and at least some of the video.

Let's find out more about navigating through cyber-space on an iPhone.

Surfin' Dude

A version of Apple's Safari Web browser is a major reason the Net is the Net on the iPhone. Safari for the Mac, and of late Windows, is one of the best Web browsers in the computer business. And in our view it has no rival as a cell phone browser.

Exploring the browser

It is worth starting our cyberexpedition with a quick tour of the Safari browser. Take a gander at Figure 10-1. Not all the browser controls found on a PC or Mac are present. Still, the iPhone's Safari has a familiar look and feel. We get to these and other controls throughout this chapter.

Address field

Go to Add Bookmark page

Reload Web page

Next Web page

Bookmarks

Pages

Previous Web page

Navigation bar

Figure 10-1: The iPhone's Safari browser.

Before plunging in, we recommend a little detour. Read the "Living on the EDGE" sidebar to find out more about the wireless networks that let you surf the Web on the iPhone in the first place.

Living on the EDGE

You can't typically make or receive phone calls on a wireless phone without tapping into a cellular network. And you can't prowl the virtual corridors of cyberspace (or send e-mail) on a mobile phone without accessing a wireless *data* network. The iPhone is compatible with two such data networks, Wi-Fi and AT&T's EDGE. (It also works with a third wireless technology called Bluetooth, addressed in Chapter 13.)

The iPhone automatically hops onto the fastest available network, which is almost always Wi-Fi. Wi-Fi is the friendly moniker applied to the far geekier *802.11* designation. And "eight-oh-two-dot-eleven" (as it is pronounced) is followed by a letter, typically (but not always) *b, g,* or *n*. So you'll see it written as 802.11b, 802.11g, and so on. The letters relate to differing technical standards that have to do with the speed and range you can expect out of the Wi-Fi configuration. But we certainly wouldn't have you lose any sleep over this, if you haven't boned up on this geeky alphabet.

For the record, the iPhone adheres to 802.11b and 802.11g standards, which means it works with most common Internet routers available to the masses and most public and private Internet *hotspots*, found at airports, colleges, coffeehouses, and elsewhere. If you have to present a password to take advantage of a for-fee hotspot, you can enter it via the iPhone's virtual keyboard.

The problem with Wi-Fi is that it is far from ubiquitous, which leads us right back to EDGE. If you're ever on a million dollar game show and have to answer the question, EDGE is shorthand for *Enhanced Datarate for GSM Evolution*. It's based on the global *GSM* phone standard.

AT&T describes EDGE as a speedy *3G,* or *third-generation,* data network, though you'll get plenty of arguments to the contrary. Some describe EDGE as a 2.5G or 2.75G network because it is far pokier than some rival high-speed data networks.

The bottom line is this: Depending on where you live or work, you may feel like you are teetering on the EDGE in terms of acceptable Internet coverage. We've used the iPhone in areas where Web pages load really slowly, not-so-vaguely reminiscent of dial-up telephone modems for your computer.

So why did Apple and AT&T choose EDGE for the iPhone? One reason is that EDGE is darn pervasive, at least according to AT&T; it says its network is available in more than 13,000 cities and towns and along 40,000 miles of highways. The 3G networks also hog more power than EDGE, a potentially serious hit on the iPhone's battery life. (Of course, Wi-Fi can put strains on a battery too.) And 3G networks weren't standardized until pretty far into iPhone's development.

There is already speculation about when Apple will unveil a true 3G-capable iPhone, but the company is characteristically mum on its future plans. Unfortunately, although Apple can fix bugs and upgrade certain iPhone features through software, they would have to introduce new hardware to take advantage of zippier networks.

Blasting off into cyberspace

So we've told you how great Web pages look on the iPhone and you're eager to get going. We won't hold you back much longer.

When you start by tapping the address field, the virtual keyboard appears. You may notice one thing about the keyboard right off the bat. Because so many Web addresses end with the suffix *.com* (pronounced "dotcom"), the virtual keyboard has a dedicated .com key. But for other common Web suffixes such as *.edu, .gov, .net,* and *.org,* you'll have to tap out all the letters.

Of equal importance, both the . (period) and the / (slash) are on the virtual keyboard, because they too are frequently entered in Web addresses.

The moment you tap a single letter, you see a list of Web addresses that match those letters. For example, if you tap the letter *E* as we did in the example in Figure 10-2, you'll see Web listings for EarthLink, and eBay, and so on. Tapping *U* or *H* instead may bring up URLs for *USA TODAY* or the *Houston Chronicle*, shameless plugs for the newspapers where Ed and Bob are columnists.

The iPhone has two ways to determine Web sites to suggest when you tap letters. One method is the Web sites you've already bookmarked from the Safari or Internet Explorer browsers on your computer (and synchronized as described in Chapter 3). More on bookmarks later in this chapter.

The second method is sites from the History list, those cyberdestinations you've recently hung your hat in. Because history repeats itself, we'll also tackle that topic later in the chapter.

Figure 10-2: Matching Web pages.

Let's open our first Web page now — and a full HTML page at that, to borrow from techie lingo:

1. **Tap the Safari icon at the bottom of the Home screen.**

   It's another member of the Fantastic Four (along with Phone, Mail, and iPod).

2. **Tap the address field (labeled in Figure 10-1).**

   If you can't see the address field, tap the status bar or scroll to the top of the screen.

3. **Begin typing the Web address, or *URL* (*Uniform Resource Locator* for you trivia buffs), on the virtual keyboard that slides up from the bottom of the screen.**

4. **Do one of the following:**

   a. **To accept one of the bookmarked (or other) sites that show up on the list, merely tap the name.**

      Safari automatically fills in the URL in the address field and takes you where you want to go.

   b. **Keep tapping the proper keyboard characters until you've entered the complete Web address for the site you have in mind, and then tap Go at the bottom-right corner of the keyboard.**

      It is not necessary to type *www* at the beginning of a URL. So to visit `www.theonion.com`, for example, entering *theonion.com* is sufficient. You are transported to the site in question.

Even though Safari on the iPhone can render Web pages the way they are meant to be displayed on a computer, every so often you may run into a site that will serve up the light, or mobile, version of the Web site, sometimes known as a WAP site. Graphics may be stripped down on such sites. Alas, the producers of these sites may be unwittingly discriminating against you for dropping in on them via a cell phone. Never mind that the cell phone in this case is an iPhone. You have our permission to berate them with letters, e-mails, and phone calls until they get with the program.

I Can See Clearly Now

Now that you know how to open up a Web page, we'll show you how radically simple it is to zoom in on the pages so you can read what you want to read and see what you want to see, without enlisting a magnifying glass.

Try these neat tricks:

- ✔ **Double-tap the screen so that that portion of the text fills up the entire screen:** It'll take just a second before the screen comes into focus. By way of example, check out Figure 10-3. It shows two views of the same *Sports Illustrated* Web page. In the first view, you see what the page looks like when you first arrive. In the second, you see how the middle column takes over the screen after you double-tapped on it. To return to the first view, double-tap the screen again.

Figure 10-3: Doing a double-tap dance zooms in and out.

- ✔ **Pinch the page:** Sliding your thumb and index finger together and then spreading them apart (or as we like to say, un-pinching) also zooms in and out of a page. Again, wait just a moment for the screen to come into focus.

- ✔ **Press down on a page and drag it in all directions, or flick through a page from top to bottom:** You are panning and scrolling, baby.

- ✔ **Rotate the iPhone to its side:** Watch what happens to the White House Web site shown in Figure 10-4. It reorients from portrait to a widescreen view. The keyboard is also wider, making it a little easier to enter a new URL.

Figure 10-4: Going wide.

Opening multiple Web pages at once

When we surf the Web on a desktop PC or laptop, we rarely go to a single Web page and call it a day. In fact, we often have multiple Web pages open at the same time. Sometimes it's because we choose to hop around the Web without closing the pages we've visited. Sometimes a link (see the next section) automatically opens a new page without shuttering the old one. (If they're advertisements, these additional pages aren't always welcome.)

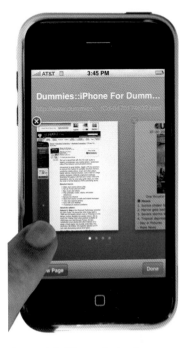

Safari on the iPhone lets you open multiple pages simultaneously. Tap the pages icon (labeled in Figure 10-1), which is on the right side of the navigation bar at the bottom of the screen, and then tap New Page on the screen that pops up next. Tap the address field and type a URL for your new page.

The number inside the pages icon lets you know how many pages are open. To see the other open pages, flick your finger to the left or right as shown in Figure 10-5. Tap a page to have it take over the full screen.

To close one of your open Web pages, tap the white x in the red circle, which appears in the upper-left corner.

Figure 10-5: All open for business.

Lovable links

Surfing the Web would be a real drag if you had to enter a URL each time you wanted to navigate from one page to another. That's why bookmarks are so useful. And it's why handy links are welcome too. Because Safari functions on the iPhone the same way browsers work on your PC or Mac, links on the iPhone pretty much behave the same way too.

Text links that transport you from one site to another are usually underlined in blue. Merely tap the link to go directly to that site.

But tapping on some other links leads to different outcomes:

 ✔ **Open a map:** Tapping on a map launches the Google Maps application that will be, um, addressed in Chapter 12.

✓ **Prepare an e-mail:** Tap an e-mail address and the iPhone opens the Mail program (see the next chapter), and pre-populates the To field with that address. The virtual keyboard is also summoned so you can add other e-mail addresses and compose a subject line and message.

✓ **Make a phone call:** Tap a phone number embedded in a Web page, and the iPhone offers to dial it for you. Just tap Call to make it happen or Cancel to forget the whole thing.

To see the URL for a link, press your finger against the link and keep it there. This is also a way to determine if a picture has a link.

Not every Web link will cooperate with the iPhone. As of this writing, the iPhone didn't support some common Web standards, notably Adobe Flash video and Java. It's a void we hope is addressed — and Apple can apply such an upgrade if it so chooses through a software update. In the meantime, if you come upon an incompatible link, nothing may happen or a message will be displayed about having to install a plug-in.

Book (mark) 'em Dano

You already know how useful bookmarks are and how you can synchronize bookmarks from the browsers on your computer. It's equally simple to bookmark a Web page directly on the iPhone:

1. **With the page you want to bookmark open, tap the + in the upper-left corner of the screen.**

   Scroll to the top of the screen if the + is not visible. The Add Bookmark screen appears, as shown in Figure 10-6, with a default name and folder location.

2. **To accept the default bookmark name and default bookmark folder, tap Save.**

3. **To change the default bookmark name, tap the x in the circle next to the name and enter the new title with the virtual keyboard. Then tap Save.**

4. **To change the location where the bookmark is saved, tap the > in the Bookmarks field and then tap the folder where you want the bookmark kept. Then tap Save.**

Figure 10-6: Turning into a bookie.

To open a bookmarked page after you've set it up, tap the bookmarks icon at the bottom of the screen (labeled in Figure 10-1) and then tap the appropriate bookmark.

If the bookmark you have in mind is buried inside a folder, tap the folder name first and then the bookmark.

Altering bookmarks

If a bookmarked site is no longer meaningful, you can change it or get rid of it :

- ✔ To remove a bookmark (or folder), tap the bookmarks icon and then tap Edit. Tap the red circle next to the bookmark you want to toss off the list and then tap Delete.

- ✔ To change a bookmark name or location, tap Edit and then tap the bookmark. The Edit Bookmark screen appears with the name, URL, and location of the bookmark already filled in. Tap the fields you want to change. In the name field, tap the x in the gray circle and then use the keyboard to enter a new title. In the location field, tap the > and scroll up or down the list until you find a new home for your bookmark.

- ✔ To create a new folder for your bookmarks, tap Edit and then tap the New Folder button. Enter the name of the new folder and choose where to put it.

- ✔ To move a bookmark up or down on a list, tap Edit and then drag the three bars to the right of the bookmark name.

Letting History repeat itself

Sometimes you want to revisit a site that you failed to bookmark. But you can't remember what the darn destination was called or what led you there in the first place. Good thing you can study the history books.

Safari records the pages you visit and keeps the logs on hand for several days. Tap the bookmarks icon, tap History, and then tap the day you think you hung out at the site. When you find it, tap the listing. You are about to make your triumphant return.

To clear your history so nobody else can trace your steps — and just what is it you are hiding? — tap Clear at the bottom of the History list. Alternately, tap Settings on the Home page, tap Safari, and then tap Clear History. In both instances, per usual, you'll have a chance to back out without wiping the slate clean.

Launching a mobile search mission

Most of us spend a lot of time on the Internet with search engines. And the search engines we summon most often are Google and Yahoo! So it goes on the iPhone.

Although you can certainly use the virtual keyboard to type google.com or yahoo.com in the Safari address field, Apple doesn't require that tedious effort. Instead, you tap into Google or Yahoo! via the dedicated search box shown in Figure 10-7. The default search engine of choice on the iPhone is Google, with Yahoo the first runner-up.

To conduct a Web search on the iPhone, tap the address field and then tap the Google (or Yahoo!) search field. Enter your search term or phrase and then tap the Google (or Yahoo!) button at the bottom-right of the keyboard to generate pages of results. Tap any search results that look promising.

To switch the search box from Google to Yahoo! and vice versa, tap Settings on the Home page, scroll down and tap Safari, tap Search Engine, and then tap to choose one search behemoth over the other.

Figure 10-7: Conducting a Google search about iPhone on the iPhone.

Smart Safari Settings

Along with the riches galore found on the Internet are places in cyberspace where you'll get hassled. Some of you may take pains to protect your privacy and maintain your security.

Let's return to Settings, by tapping the Settings icon on the Home page. Now tap Safari.

We've already discovered how to change the default search engine and clear the record of the sites we've visited through Settings. Now let's see what else we can do:

✐ **Clear cookies**: We're not talking about crumbs you may have accidentally dropped on the iPhone. Cookies are tiny bits of information that a
Web site places on the iPhone when you visit so that they'll recognize
you when you return. You need not assume the worst; most cookies are
benign. But if this concept wigs you out, you can do a few things.

Tap Clear Cookies at the bottom of the screen and then tap it again
(instead of tapping Cancel). Separately, tap Accept Cookies and then tap
Never. Theoretically, you will never receive cookies on the iPhone again.
A good middle ground is to accept cookies only from the sites you visit.
To do so, tap From Visited. You can also tap Always to accept cookies
from all sites.

If you don't set the iPhone to accept cookies, certain Web pages won't
load properly.

Tap Safari to return to the main Safari settings page.

✐ **Clear the cache:** The cache stores content from some Web pages so
they load faster the next time you stop by. Tap Clear Cache and then tap
Clear Cache again on the next screen to, you guessed it, clear the cache.

✐ **Turn JavaScript on or off:** This setting is on when the blue On button is
showing and off when the white Off button is showing. Programmers use
JavaScript to add various functionality to Web pages, from displaying
the date and time to changing images when you mouse over them.
However, some security risks have also been associated with JavaScript.

✐ **Turn plug-ins on or off:** These are typically associated with certain
types of video.

✐ **Block pop-ups:** Pop-ups are those Web pages that show up whether you
want them to or not. Often they are annoying advertisements. But at
some sites you'll welcome the appearance of pop-ups, so remember to
turn blocking off under such circumstances.

Taming Safari is just the start of exploiting the Internet on the iPhone. In
upcoming chapters, you discover how to master e-mail, maps, and more.

The E-Mail Must Get Through

You saw how well your iPhone sends SMS text messages in Chapter 5. But SMS text messages aren't the iPhone's only written communication trick, not by a long shot. One of the niftiest things your iPhone can do is send and receive real, honest-to-gosh e-mail, using Mail, its modern e-mail application. It's designed not only to send and receive text e-mail messages, but also to handle rich HTML e-mail messages — formatted e-mail messages complete with font and type styles and embedded graphics.

Furthermore, your iPhone can read several types of file attachments, including PDF, Microsoft Word, and Microsoft Excel documents. Better still, all this sending and receiving of text, graphics, and documents can happen in the background, so you can surf the Web or talk to a friend while your iPhone quietly and efficiently handles your e-mail behind the scenes.

Prep Work: Setting Up Your Accounts

First things first. To use Mail you need an e-mail address. If you have broadband Internet access (that is, a cable modem or DSL), you probably received one or more e-mail addresses when you signed up. If you are one of the handful of readers who don't already have an e-mail account, you can get one for free from Yahoo! (http://mail.yahoo.com), Google (http://mail.google.com), and many other service providers.

©iStockphoto.com/Chad Anderson

Using Yahoo mail has a small advantage. The free accounts it offers are known as "push" e-mail, which means your messages are delivered to your iPhone as soon as they are received by the mail server. With other e-mail accounts, your iPhone doesn't check for new messages until you ask it to.

Many (if not all) free e-mail providers add a small bit of advertising at the end of your outgoing messages. If you'd rather not be a billboard for your e-mail provider, either use the address(es) that came with your broadband Internet access (*yourname*@comcast.net, *yourname*@att.net, and so on) or pay a few dollars a month for a premium e-mail account that doesn't tack advertising (or anything else) onto your messages.

Set up your account the easy way

Remember way back in Chapter 3, you had the option of automatically syncing the e-mail accounts on your computer with your iPhone? If you chose to do so, your e-mail accounts should be configured on your iPhone already. You can go directly to the "Darling, You Send Me (E-Mail)" section.

If you didn't choose that option but would like to set up your account the easy way now, go back to Chapter 3 and reread that section, sync your iPhone, and then you, too, can go directly to the "Darling, You Send Me (E-Mail)" section.

Set up your account the less easy way

If you don't want to sync the e-mail accounts on your computer, you can set up an e-mail account on your iPhone manually. It's not quite as easy as clicking a box and syncing your iPhone, but it's not rocket science either.

If you have no mail accounts on your iPhone, the first time you launch Mail you'll be walked through the following procedure. If instead you have one or more mail accounts on your iPhone already and want to add a new account manually, start by tapping Settings on the Home screen, and then tap Mail, Accounts, and Add Accounts.

Either way, you should now be staring at the Add Account screen, which is shown in Figure 11-1. Proceed to one of the next two sections, depending on your e-mail account.

Setting up a mail account with Yahoo!, Google, .Mac, or AOL

If your account is with Yahoo!, Google, .Mac, or AOL, tap the appropriate button on the Add Account screen now. If your account is with a provider other than these four, tap the Other button and skip ahead to the next section.

Enter your name, e-mail address, and password, as shown in Figure 11-2. There's a field for a description of this account (such as work or personal), but it's optional so feel free to leave it blank if you want.

Tap the Save button in the top-right corner of the screen. You're finished. That's all there is to setting up your account.

Setting up an account with another provider

If your e-mail account is with a provider other than Yahoo!, Google, .Mac, or AOL, you have a bit more work ahead of you to set up an account.

Figure 11-1: Tap a button to add an account.

You're going to need a bunch of information about your e-mail account that you may not know or have handy.

We suggest that you scan the following instructions, note the items you don't know, and go find them out before you continue. To find them, look at the documentation you received when you signed up for your e-mail account or visit the account provider's Web site and search there. If you work in a business and are trying to access your business e-mail, try contacting your company's IT (information technology) person or department to get the necessary information.

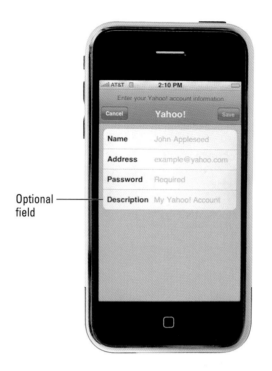

Optional
field

Figure 11-2: Just fill 'em in, tap Save, and you're ready to rock.

Now here's how you set up an account:

1. **On the Add Account screen, tap the Other button.**

2. **Tap the button at the top of the screen that denotes the type of e-mail server this account uses: IMAP, POP, or Exchange, as shown in Figure 11-3.**

3. **Enter the e-mail address for this account.**

4. **(Optional) Enter a description of this account (such as *work* or *personal*).**

5. **Enter the Internet host name for your incoming mail server, which should look something like mail.*providername*.com.**

6. **Enter the Internet host name for your outgoing mail server, which should look something like smtp.*providername*.com.**

7. **Enter your user name and password for both servers.**

8. **Tap the Save button in the upper-right corner to create the account.**

Some outgoing mail servers don't need your user name and password. The fields for these items on your iPhone note that they are optional. Still, we suggest that you fill them in anyway. It will save you from having to add them later if your outgoing mail server *does* require an account name and password, which many do these days.

If your mail server is an Exchange server, it has to be configured for IMAP. Don't worry if you don't know what that means. Because Exchange servers are almost always deployed in large organizations, it's more than likely you have an IT person or department that can help. Just remember that if your Exchange server *isn't* set up for IMAP, you won't be able to use this account with your iPhone.

Indeed, around the time of the iPhone's early summer 2007 launch, many employers were cautiously taking a wait-and-see attitude before letting the troops send and receive company e-mail on the device. Apple has been working with major corporations on pilot programs to address any e-mail concerns they might have. By the time you read this, many more companies may have embraced e-mail on the iPhone.

Figure 11-3: If you're not a Yahoo!, Google, .Mac, or AOL user you have slightly more fields to fill in before you can rock.

Darling, You Send Me (E-Mail)

Now that your account or accounts are set up, let's look at how to use your iPhone to send e-mail.

Makin' messages

There are several subspecies of messages: pure text, text with a photo, a partially finished message you want to save and complete later (called a draft), a reply to an incoming message, forwarding an incoming message to someone else, and so on. Let's examine these subsets one at a time.

Sending an all-text message

To compose a new e-mail message, tap Mail on your Home screen. You should see a screen that looks pretty much like the one in Figure 11-4.

Tap to see other e-mail accounts

Number of unread messages

Name of this e-mail account

New message

Figure 11-4: The mailboxes screen.

Don't worry if yours doesn't look exactly like this or if your folders have different names.

Now to create a new message:

1. **Tap the new message button (labeled in Figure 11-4) in the lower-right corner of the screen.**

   A screen like the one shown in Figure 11-5 appears.

2. **Type the names or e-mail addresses of the recipients in the To or CC (carbon copy) field, or tap the + button on the right side of the To or CC field to choose a contact from your iPhone's address book.**

   If you start typing an e-mail address, e-mail addresses that match what you've typed appear in a list below the To or CC field. If the correct one is in the list, tap it to use it.

3. **Type a subject in the Subject field.**

   The subject is optional but it's considered poor form to send an e-mail message without one.

4. **Type your message in the message
   area.**

   The message area is immediately
   below the Subject field.

5. **Tap the Send button in the top-right
   corner of the screen.**

Your message will wing its way to its recipients almost immediately. If you are not in
range of a Wi-Fi network or the AT&T EDGE
data network when you tap Send, the message is sent next time you are in range
of either network.

Figure 11-5: The new message
appears ready for you to start typing
the recipient's name.

Sending a photo with a text message

Sometimes a picture is worth a thousand
words. When that's the case, here's how
to send an e-mail message with a photo
enclosed.

Tap the Photos icon on the Home screen
and then find the photo you want to send.
Tap the button that looks like a little rectangle with a curved arrow springing
out of it in the bottom-left corner of the screen, and then tap the Email Photo
button.

An e-mail message appears on the screen with the photo already attached.
Just address the message and type whatever text you like, as you did for an
all-text message in the preceding section, and then tap the Send button.

Saving an e-mail message so you can send it later

Sometimes you start an e-mail message but don't have time to finish it. When
that happens you can save it as a draft and finish it some other time.

Here's how: Start an e-mail message as described in one of the two previous sections. When you're ready to save it as a draft, tap the Cancel button in the top-left corner of the screen. Now tap the Save button if you want to save this message as a draft and complete it at another time. If you tap the Cancel button, you'll cancel the cancel command and go right back to the message and can continue working on it now.

If you tap the Don't Save button, the message disappears immediately without a second chance. Don't tap Don't Save unless you mean it.

To work on the message again, tap the Drafts mailbox. A list of all the messages you've saved as drafts appears. Tap the one you want to work on and it reappears on the screen. When you're finished, you can tap Send to send it, or tap Cancel to save it as a draft again.

The number of drafts appears on the right of the Drafts folder, the same way that the number of unread messages appears on the right of other mail folders such as your Inbox.

Replying to or forwarding an e-mail message

When you receive a message and want to reply to it, open the message and then tap the reply/reply all/forward button, which looks like a curved arrow at the bottom of the screen, as shown in Figure 11-6. Then tap either the Reply, Reply All, or Forward button.

The Reply button creates a blank e-mail message addressed to the sender of the original message. The Reply All button creates a blank e-mail

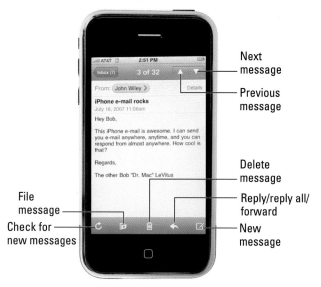

Figure 11-6: Reading and managing an e-mail message.

message addressed to the sender and all other recipients of the original message. In both cases the subject is retained with a *Re:* prefix added. So if the original subject was *iPhone Tips,* the reply's subject would be *Re: iPhone Tips.*

Tapping the Forward button creates an unaddressed e-mail message that contains the text of the original message. Add the e-mail address(es) of the person or people you want to forward the message to, and then tap Send. In this case, instead of a *Re:* prefix, the subject is preceded by *Fwd:*. So this time the subject would be *Fwd: iPhone Tips.*

You can edit the subject line of a reply or a forwarded message or edit the body text of a forwarded message the same way you would edit any other text. It's usually considered good form to leave the subject lines alone (with the *Re:* or *Fwd:* prefix intact), but there may be times when you want to change them. Now you know that you can.

To send your reply or forwarded message, tap the Send button as usual.

Settings for sending e-mail

Four settings involve sending e-mail. Here's what they do and where to find them:

   ✔ **To hear an alert when you successfully send a message:** Tap the Sound icon on the Home screen, and then turn on the Sent Mail setting. If you want to change other settings, tap the Settings button in the top-left corner of the screen. If you're finished setting settings, tap the Home button on the front of your iPhone.

The preceding paragraph is similar for all of the settings I discuss in this section and later sections, so I won't repeat them again. To summarize, if you want to continue using settings, you tap whichever button appears in the top-left corner of the screen — sometimes it's called Settings, or Mail, or Mailboxes, or something else. The point is that the top-left button always returns you to the previous screen so you can change other settings. And the same applies to pressing the Home button on the front of your iPhone when you're finished setting a setting. That always saves the change you've just made and returns you to the Home screen.

   ✔ **To add a signature line, phrase, or block of text to every e-mail message you send:** Tap the Settings icon on the Home screen, tap Mail, and then tap Signature. The default signature is *Sent from my iPhone.* You can add text before or after it, or delete it and type something else. Your signature is now affixed to the end of all of your outgoing e-mail.

   ✔ **To have your iPhone send you a copy of every message you send:** Tap the Settings icon on the Home screen, tap Mail, and then turn on the Always Cc Myself setting.

✔ **To set the default e-mail account for sending e-mail from the Photos or Maps applications:** Tap the Settings icon on the Home screen, tap Mail, and then tap Default Account. Tap the account you want to use as the default. Note that this setting applies only if you have more than one e-mail account on your iPhone.

And that's what you need to know about settings that apply to sending mail.

See Me, Read Me, File Me, Delete Me: Working with Messages

The other half of the mail equation is receiving and reading the stuff. Fortunately, you've already done most of the heavy lifting when you set up your e-mail accounts. Getting and reading your mail is a piece of cake.

You can tell when you have unread mail by looking at the Mail icon, in the bottom row of your Home screen. The number of unread messages appears in a little red circle on the top-right of the icon.

Reading messages

To read your mail, tap the Mail icon on the Home screen. The mailboxes list appears, and the Inbox in that list displays the number of unread messages in a blue oval to the right of its name.

If you have more than one e-mail account, you may have to tap the Mailboxes button in the upper-left corner and then choose the appropriate e-mail account before you see the Inbox with the unread messages.

To see the list of unread messages, tap Inbox in the list of mailboxes and then tap a message to read it. When a message is on the screen, buttons for managing incoming messages appear below it (refer to Figure 11-6).

Managing messages

When a message is on your screen, you can do the following in addition to reading it (all buttons are labeled in Figure 11-6):

✔ View the next message by tapping the next message button.

✔ View the previous message by tapping the previous message button.

✓ Check for new messages by tapping the check for new messages button.

✓ File this message in another folder by tapping the file message button. When the list of folders appears, tap the folder where you want to file the message.

✓ Delete this message by tapping the delete message button.

✓ Reply, reply to all, or forward this message (as discussed previously) by tapping the reply/reply all/forward button.

✓ Create a new e-mail message by tapping the new message button.

You can delete e-mail messages without opening them in two ways:

✓ Swipe left or right across the message and then tap the red Delete button that appears to the right of the message.

✓ Tap the Edit button in the upper-left corner of the screen, tap the red minus (–) button to the left of the message, and then tap the red Delete button that appears to the right of the message.

Don't grow too attached to attachments

Your iPhone can even receive e-mail messages with attachments in a wide variety of file formats. What file formats does the iPhone support? Glad you asked. It can read and display .c, .cpp, .diff, .doc, .docx, .h, .hpp, .htm, .html, .m, .mm, .patch, .pdf, .txt, .xls, and xlsx.

If the attachment is a file format not supported by the iPhone (for example, a Photoshop .psd file), you'll see the name of the file but you won't be able to open it on your iPhone.

Here's how to read an attachment:

1. **Open the mail message containing the attachment.**

2. **Tap the attachment (it appears at the bottom of the message so you'll probably need to scroll down to see it).**

   The attachment downloads to your iPhone and opens automatically, as shown in Figure 11-7.

3. **Read the attachment.**

4. **Tap the Message button in the upper-left corner of the screen to return to the message text.**

More things you can do with messages

But wait! You can do even more with your incoming e-mail messages:

✔ To see all the recipients of a message, tap the word Details (displayed in blue) to the right of the sender's name.

If all recipients are displayed, the word in blue will be Hide rather than Details. Tap it to hide all names but the sender's.

✔ To add an e-mail recipient or sender to your contacts, tap the name or e-mail address at the top of the message and then tap either Create New Contact or Add to Existing Contact.

✔ To mark a message as unread, tap Mark as Unread, which appears near the top of each message in blue with a blue dot to its left. When you do, the message will again be included in the unread message count on the Mail icon on your Home screen and its mailbox and will again have a blue dot next to it in the message list for that mailbox.

Figure 11-7: Text from a Microsoft Word file that was attached to an incoming e-mail message.

✔ To zoom in, double-tap the place you want to zoom in on. Double-tap again to zoom out.

For more precise control over zooming, pinch and un-pinch instead of double-tapping.

✔ To follow a link in a message, tap the link. Links are typically displayed in blue. If the link is a URL, Safari opens and displays the Web page. If the link is a phone number, the Phone application opens and offers to dial the number. If the link is a Map, Maps opens and displays the location. And last but not least, if the link is an e-mail address, a new pre-addressed blank e-mail message is created.

If the link opens Safari, Phone, or Maps and you want to return to your e-mail, press the Home button on the front of your iPhone and then tap the Mail icon.

Setting your message and account settings

Our last lesson on Mail involves more settings, this time settings that affect viewing and checking e-mail and messages that deal with your e-mail accounts themselves.

Checking and viewing e-mail settings

Seven settings involve checking and viewing e-mail. You might want to modify one or more, so here's what they do and where to find them:

- **To set how often the iPhone checks for new messages:** Tap the Settings icon on the Home screen, tap Mail, and then tap Auto-Check. Your choices are Manual, Every 15 Minutes, Every 30 Minutes, or Every Hour. Tap the one you prefer.

   If you have Yahoo! e-mail, this setting is irrelevant. Your messages are sent to your iPhone automatically as soon as they hit the Yahoo! mail server.

- **To hear an alert sound when you receive a new message:** Tap the Sound icon on the Home screen, and then turn on the New Mail setting.

- **To set the number of recent messages that appears in your Inbox:** Tap the Settings icon on the Home screen, tap Mail, and then tap Show. Your choices are 25, 50, 75, 100, or 200. Tap the number you prefer.

   You can always see more messages in your Inbox regardless of this setting by scrolling all the way to the bottom and tapping Download More.

- **To set the number of lines of each message that are displayed in the message list:** Tap the Settings icon on the Home screen, tap Mail, tap Preview, and then choose a number. Your choices are 0, 1, 2, 3, 4, or 5 lines of text. The more lines of text you display in the list, the fewer messages you can see at a time without scrolling. Think before you choose 4 or 5.

- **To set the font size for messages:** Tap the Settings icon on the Home screen, tap Mail, and then tap Minimum Font Size. Your options are Small, Medium, Large, Extra Large, or Giant. Use trial and error to find out which size you prefer. Choose one and then read a message. If it's not just right, choose a different size. Repeat until you're happy.

- **To set whether or not the iPhone shows the To and Cc labels in message lists:** Tap the Settings icon on the Home screen, tap Mail, and then turn the Show To/Cc Label setting on or off.

✔ **To turn the Ask Before Deleting warning on or off:** Tap the Settings icon on the Home screen, tap Mail, and then turn the Ask Before Deleting setting on or off. If this setting is turned on, you need to tap the trash can icon at the bottom of the screen and then tap the red Delete button to confirm the deletion. When it's turned off, tapping the trash can icon deletes the message and you never see a red Delete button.

Altering account settings

The last set of settings we explore deals with your e-mail accounts. Most of you will never need most of these settings, but we'd be remiss if we didn't at least mention them briefly. So here they are, whether you need 'em or not:

✔ **To stop using an e-mail account:** Tap the Settings icon on the Home screen, tap Mail, and then tap the account name. Tap the switch to turn off the account.

This setting doesn't delete the account; it only hides it from view and stops it from sending or checking e-mail until you turn it on again.

✔ **To delete an e-mail account:** Tap the Settings icon on the Home screen, tap Mail, and then tap the account name. Scroll to the very bottom and tap the red button that says Delete Account. You'll be given a chance to reconsider. Tap Delete Account if you're sure you want this account blown away or Cancel if you change your mind and want to keep it.

The last four settings are somewhat advanced and are all reached the same way: Tap the Settings icon on the Home screen, tap Mail, and then tap the name of the account you want to work with. Then:

✔ **To set how long until deleted messages are removed permanently from your iPhone:** Tap Advanced, and then tap Remove. Your choices are Never, After One Day, After One Week, or After One Month. Tap the choice you prefer.

✔ **To set whether drafts, sent messages, and deleted messages are stored on your iPhone or on your mail server:** Tap Advanced, and then choose the setting (Stored on iPhone or Stored on Server) for Drafts, Sent Messages, and Deleted Messages. If you choose to store any or all of them on the server, you won't be able to see them unless you have an Internet connection (Wi-Fi or EDGE). If you choose to store them on your iPhone, they'll always be available whether or not you have Internet access.

We strongly recommend that you not change these next two items unless you know exactly what you're doing and why. If you're having problems with sending or receiving mail, start by contacting your ISP (Internet service provider), e-mail provider, or corporate IT person or department. Then, only change these settings if they tell you to.

✏ **To reconfigure mail server settings:** Tap Host Name, User Name, or Password in the Incoming Mail Server or Outgoing Mail Server section of the account settings screen and make your changes.

✏ **To adjust Incoming or Outgoing SSL, Authentication, or IMAP Path settings:** Tap Advanced, and then tap the appropriate item and make the necessary changes.

And that, as they say in baseball, retires the side. You are now fully qualified to set up e-mail accounts and send and receive e-mail on your iPhone.

12

Monitoring Maps, Scrutinizing Stocks, and Watching Weather

In This Chapter

▶ Mapping your route with Maps
▶ Getting quotes with Stocks
▶ Watching the weather with Weather

*I*n this chapter we look at three of the iPhone's Internet-enabled applications: Maps, Stocks, and Weather. We call them *Internet-enabled* because they display information collected over your Internet connection — whether Wi-Fi or EDGE — in real (or in the case of Stocks, near-real) time.

Maps Are Where It's At . . .

Maps has turned out to be the sleeper hit of our iPhone experience and an application we both use more than we expected. That's because it's so darn handy. With Maps, you can quickly and easily find nearby restaurants and businesses, get turn-by-turn driving instructions from any address to any other address, and see real-time traffic information for any location.

©iStockphoto.com/Yuri Hnilazub

Finding a person, place, or thing with Maps

Tap the Maps icon on the Home screen, and then tap the search field at the top of the screen to make the keyboard appear. Now type what you're looking for. You can search for addresses, zip codes, intersections, towns, landmarks, businesses by category and by name, and combinations, such as *New York, NY 10022, pizza 60645* or *Auditorium Shores Austin TX.*

If the letters you type match names in your Contacts list, the matching contacts appear in a list below the search field. Tap a name to see a map of that contact's location. Maps is smart about it, too; it displays only the names of contacts with a street address.

When you finish typing, tap Search. After a few seconds, a map appears. If you searched for a single location, it is marked with a single pushpin. If you searched for a category (*pizza 60645,* for example), you see multiple pushpins, one for each matching location, as shown in Figure 12-1.

So that's how to find just about anything with Maps. Now let's look at some of the ways you can use what you find.

Views, zooms, and pans

Let's start by finding out how to work with what you see on the screen. Three views are available at any time: Map, Satellite, and List. (Figure 12-1 shows the Map view.) Select the one you want by tapping its button at the bottom of the screen.

Figure 12-1: Search for *pizza 60645* and you see pushpins for all nearby pizza joints.

In Map or Satellite view, you can zoom to see more or less of the map, or scroll (pan) to see what's above, below, or to the left or right of what's on the screen:

   ✔ **To zoom out:** Pinch the map or double-tap using two fingers. To zoom out even more, pinch or double-tap using two fingers again.

   This is a new concept. To double-tap with two fingers, merely tap twice in rapid succession with two fingers rather than the usual one finger. (That's a total of four taps, two taps per finger.)

   ✔ **To zoom in:** Un-pinch the map or double-tap (the usual way — with just one finger) the spot you want to zoom in on. Un-pinch or double-tap with one finger again to zoom in even more.

An un-pinch is the opposite of a pinch. Start with your thumb and a finger together and then flick them apart.

You can also un-pinch with two fingers or two thumbs, one from each hand, but you'll probably find that a single-handed pinch and un-pinch is handier.

✔ **To scroll:** Flick or drag up, down, left, or right.

Maps and contacts

Maps and contacts go together like peanut butter and jelly. For example, if you want to see a map of a contact's street address, tap the little bookmark icon in the search field, tap the Contacts button at the bottom of the screen, and then tap the contact's name.

Or type the first few letters of the contact's name in the search field and then tap the name in the list that automatically appears below the search field.

After you find a location by typing an address into Maps, you can add that location to one of your contacts. Or you can create a new contact with a location you've found. To do either, tap the location's pushpin on the map, and then tap the little > in a blue circle to the right of the location's name or description, as shown in Figure 12-2, to display its Info screen as shown in Figure 12-3.

Figure 12-2: Tap here to display info about a location.

Now tap either the Create New Contact button or the Add to Existing Contact button on the Info screen. You'll probably have to scroll to the bottom of the Info screen to see these buttons (shown on the right in Figure 12-3).

You work with your contacts by tapping the Phone icon on your Home screen, and then tapping the Contacts icon at the bottom of the Phone screen.

You can also get driving directions from any location including a contact's address to any other location including another contact's address. You'll see how to do that in the "Smart map tricks" section.

Figure 12-3: The unscrolled Info screen for Gulliver's Pizza (left)
and the same screen when you scroll to the bottom (right).

Timesaving map tools

Maps offers three tools that can save you from having to type the same locations over and over again. All three appear in the Bookmarks screen, which is
displayed when you tap the little blue bookmark icon on the right side of any
search field.

At the bottom of the screen you'll find three buttons: Bookmarks, Recents,
and Contacts. Here's the lowdown.

Bookmarks

Bookmarks in the Maps application work like bookmarks in Safari. When you
have a location you want to save as a bookmark so you can reuse it later
without typing a single character, tap the little > in a blue circle to the right of
its name or description to display the Info screen for that location. Tap the
Add to Bookmarks button on the Info screen. (You'll probably have to scroll
down the Info screen to see the Add to Bookmarks button.)

Once you add a location to your Bookmarks list, you can recall it at any time.
To do so, tap the bookmarks icon in any search field, tap the Bookmarks
button at the bottom of the screen, and then tap the bookmark name to see a
map of it.

The first things you should bookmark are your home and work address and your zip codes. These are things you'll be using all the time with Maps, so you might as well bookmark them now to avoid typing them over and over.

Use zip code bookmarks to find nearby businesses. Choose the zip code bookmark, and then type what you're looking for, such as *78729 pizza*, *60645 gas station*, or *90201 Starbucks*.

To manage your bookmarks, first tap the Edit button in the top-left corner of the Bookmarks screen. Then:

- ✔ **To move a bookmark up or down in the Bookmarks list:** Drag the little icon with three gray bars that appears to the right of the bookmark upward to move the bookmark higher in the list or downward to move the bookmark lower in the list.

- ✔ **To delete a bookmark from the Bookmarks list:** Tap the minus sign to the left of the bookmark's name.

When you're finished using bookmarks, tap the Done button in the top-right corner of the Bookmarks screen to return to the map.

Recents

Maps automatically keeps track of every location you've searched for in its Recents list. To see this list, tap the bookmarks icon in any search field, and then tap the Recents button at the bottom of the screen. To see a map of a recent item, tap the item's name.

To clear the Recents list, tap the Clear button in the top-left corner of the screen, and then tap the Clear All Recents button.

When you're finished using the Recents list, tap the Done button in the top-right corner of the screen to return to the map.

Contacts

To see a map of a contact's location, tap the bookmarks icon in any search field, and then tap the Contacts button at the bottom of the screen. To see a map of a contact's location, tap the contact's name in the list.

To limit the Contacts list to specific groups (assuming you have some groups in your Contacts list), tap the Groups button in the top-left corner of the screen and then tap the name of the group. Now only contacts in this group are displayed in the list.

When you're finished using the Contacts list, tap the Done button in the top-right corner of the screen to return to the map.

Smart map tricks

The Maps application has more tricks up its sleeve. Here are a few nifty features you may find useful.

Get route maps and driving directions

You can get route maps and driving directions to any location from any location in a couple of ways.

One way is to tap a pushpin on a map, and then tap the little > in a blue circle to the right of the name or description to display the item's Info screen, as shown in Figures 12-2 and 12-3. Now tap the Directions to Here or Directions from Here button to get directions to or from that location, respectively.

If you're looking at a map screen, there's another way to get directions. Tap the little up and down arrow icon at the bottom-left corner of the map screen. The Start and End fields appear at the top of the screen.

Type the starting and ending points, as shown in Figure 12-4 (or choose them from your bookmarks, recent maps, or contacts if you prefer). If you want to swap the starting and ending locations, tap the little swirly arrow button to the left of the Start and End fields.

When the start and end locations are correct, tap the Route button in the bottom-right corner of the screen and the route map appears, as shown in Figure 12-5.

Figure 12-4: Type a starting and ending location.

If you need to change the start or end location, tap the Edit button in the top-left corner. If everything looks right, tap the Start button in the top-right corner to receive turn-by-turn driving directions, as shown in Figure 12-6.

When you're finished with the step-by-step directions, tap the little up and down arrows icon in the bottom-left corner to return to the regular map screen.

Figure 12-5: The route map for the start and end locations shown in Figure 12-4.

Figure 12-6: The first step in the step-by-step driving directions for the route shown in Figure 12-5.

Get traffic info in real time

You can find out the traffic conditions for whatever map you're viewing by tapping the little car icon in the bottom-right of the screen. When you do, major roadways are color-coded to inform you of the current traffic speed. Here's the key:

- Green: 50 or more miles per hour
- Yellow: 25–50 miles per hour
- Red: Under 25 miles per hour
- Gray: No data available at this time

Traffic info doesn't work in every location, but the only way to find out is to give it a try. If no color codes appear, assume that it doesn't work for that particular location.

More about the Info screen

If a location has a little > in a blue circle to the right of its name or description (refer to Figure 12-2), you can tap it to see the location's Info screen.

You've already seen that you can get directions to or from that location, add the location to your bookmarks or contacts, or create a new contact from it, but there are still two more things you can do with a location from its Info screen:

- Tap its phone number to call it
- Tap its URL to launch Safari and view its Web site

Taking Stock with Stocks

Stocks is another Internet-enabled application on your iPhone. It's a one-trick pony, but if you need its trick — information about specific stocks — it's a winner.

Every time you open the Stocks application by tapping its icon on the Home screen, it displays the latest price for your stocks, with two provisos:

- The quotes may be delayed by up to 20 minutes.
- The quotes are updated only if your iPhone can connect to the Internet via either Wi-Fi or the AT&T EDGE data network.

So tap that Stocks icon and let's take a peek.

The first time you open Stocks you'll see information for the Dow Jones Industrial Average (^DJI), Apple (APPL), Google (GOOG), Yahoo (YHOO), and AT&T (T). Because the chances of you owning that exact group of stocks are slim, let's look at how you can add your own stocks and delete any or all of the default stocks.

Here's how to add a stock:

1. **Tap the *i* button in the bottom-right corner of the initial Stocks screen.**

   The *i* is for info.

2. **Tap the + button in the top-left corner of the Stocks screen.**

3. **Type a stock symbol, or a company, index, or fund name.**

4. **Tap the Search button.**

   Stocks finds the company or companies that match your search request.

5. **Tap the one you want to add.**

   Repeat Steps 4 and 5 until you're through adding stocks. In Figure 12-7, we added John Wiley & Sons (JW-A).

6. **Tap the Done button in the top-right corner.**

And here's how to delete a stock:

1. **Tap the *i* button in the bottom-right corner of the initial Stocks screen.**

Figure 12-7: The Stocks screen.

2. **Tap the – button to the left of the stock's name.**

3. **Tap the Delete button that appears to the right of the stock's name.**

   Repeat Steps 2 and 3 until all unwanted stocks have been deleted.

4. **Tap the Done button.**

That's all there is to adding and deleting stocks.

Here are a few more things you can do with Stocks. By default, Stocks displays the change in a stock's price in dollars. You can see the change expressed as a percentage in two ways. The easy way is to tap the number next to any stock (green numbers are positive; red numbers are negative). That toggles the display for all stocks. So if they're currently displayed as dollars, tapping any one of them switches them to percent and vice versa.

The second way accomplishes the same thing, but takes more steps. Tap the *i* button in the bottom-right corner of the initial Stocks screen. Tap the % or Numbers button at the bottom of the screen. The numbers are displayed in the manner you choose. Tap the Done button in the top-right corner.

Now refer back to Figure 12-7 and note the chart at the bottom of the window. At the top of the chart, you see a bunch of numbers and letters, namely 1d, 1w, 1m, 3m, 6m, 1y, and 2y. They are buttons you can tap to change the time period shown on the chart. They stand for 1 day, 1 week, 1 month, 3 months, 6 months, 1 year, and 2 years, respectively. Tap one of them and the chart reflects that period of time.

Finally, to look up additional information about a stock at Yahoo.com, first tap the stock's name to select it, and then tap the Y! button in the lower-left corner of the screen. Safari launches and displays the Yahoo.com finance page for that stock, as shown in Figure 12-8.

Figure 12-8: The Yahoo.com finance page for Apple (APPL).

Weather Watching

Weather is a simple application that provides you with the current weather forecast for the city or cities of your choice. By default you see a six-day forecast for the chosen city, as shown in Figure 12-9.

If the background for the forecast is blue, as shown in Figure 12-9, it's daytime (between 6 a.m. and 6 p.m.) in that city; if it's a deep purple, it's nighttime (between 6 p.m. and 6 a.m.).

To add a city, first tap the *i* button in the bottom-right corner. Tap the + button in the upper-left corner and then type a city and state or zip code. Tap the Search button in the bottom-right corner of the screen. Tap the name of the found city. Add as many cities as you want this way.

To delete a city, tap the *i* button in the bottom-right corner. Tap the red – button to the left of its name, and then tap the Delete button that appears to the right of its name.

You can also choose between Fahrenheit and Celsius on this screen by tapping either the °F or °C button near the bottom of the screen.

When you're finished, tap the Done button in the top-right corner of the screen.

Figure 12-9: The six-day forecast for Indianapolis, IN.

If you have added more than one city to Weather, you can switch between them by flicking your finger across the screen to the left or the right.

See the seven little dots — one white and six gray — at the bottom of the screen in Figure 12-9? They denote the number of stored cities (which is seven in the figure).

Last but not least, to see detailed weather information about a city at Yahoo.com, tap the Y! button in the lower-left corner of the screen. Safari launches and displays the Yahoo.com weather page for the current city, as shown in Figure 12-10.

Figure 12-10: Detailed weather on Yahoo.com is just a tap away.

Part V
The Undiscovered iPhone

The 5th Wave   By Rich Tennant

©RICHTENNANT

Cell Phone

"This model comes with a particularly useful function – a simulated static button for breaking out of long-winded conversations."

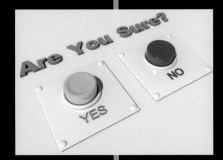

*T*his part is where we show you what's under the hood and how to configure your iPhone to your liking. Then we look at the things to do if your iPhone ever becomes recalcitrant.

In Chapter 13 we explore every single iPhone setting that's not discussed in depth elsewhere in the book. iPhone offers dozens of different preferences and settings you can customize to make your iPhone your very own; by the time you finish with Chapter 13, you'll know how to customize every part of your iPhone that *can* be customized.

iPhones are well-behaved little beasts for the most part, except when they're not. Like the little girl with the little curl, when they're good they're very very good, but when they're bad they're horrid. So Chapter 14 is your comprehensive guide to troubleshooting for the iPhone. It details what to do when almost anything goes wrong, offering step-by-step instructions for specific situations as well as a plethora of tips and techniques you can try if something else goes awry. You may never need Chapter 14 (and we hope you won't), but you'll be very glad we put it here if your iPhone ever goes wonky on you.

Photo credits:
©iStockphoto.com/Kirill Roslyakov (Top)
©iStockphoto.com/kutay tanir (Middle)
©iStockphoto.com/Chad Anderson (Bottom)

Setting You Straight on Settings

Are you a control freak? The type of person who must have it your way? Boy have you have landed in the right chapter.

Throughout this book we've had an occasion to drop in on Settings, kind of the makeover factory for the iPhone. For example, we've come to Settings (by tapping its Home screen icon) to set ringtones, change the phone's background or wallpaper, and specify Google or Yahoo! as the search engine of choice. We've also altered security settings in Safari and tailored e-mail to our liking, among other modifications.

Note: Settings on the iPhone is roughly analogous to the Control Panel in Windows and System Preferences on a Mac.

Because we've covered some settings elsewhere, we won't dwell on every setting here. But there's plenty still to discover to help you make the iPhone your own.

©iStockphoto.com/DSGpro

Sky-High Settings

When you first arrive in Settings you see the scrollable list shown in Figure 13-1. In all but airplane mode at the very top of the list, a greater than symbol (>) appears to the right of each listing. That tells you that the listing has a bunch of options. You tap the > symbol throughout this chapter to check out those options.

Figure 13-1: Presenting your list of Settings.

Airplane mode

Using a cell phone on an airplane is a no-no. But there's nothing verboten about using an iPod on a plane to listen to music, watch videos, and peek at pictures. At least once you've reached cruising altitude.

So how do you take advantage of the iPhone's built-in iPod (among other capabilities) while temporarily turning off its phone, e-mail, and Internet functions? By turning on airplane mode.

To do so, merely tap Airplane Mode on the Settings screen so that On rather than Off is displayed.

That act disables each of the iPhone's wireless radios: Wi-Fi, cell phone, and Bluetooth. While in airplane mode, you won't be able to make or receive calls, surf the Web, watch YouTube, or do anything else that requires an Internet connection. The good news is that airplane mode will keep your battery running longer — particularly useful if the flight you're on is taking you halfway around the world.

The appearance of a tiny airplane icon in the status bar at the upper left reminds you that airplane mode is turned on. Just remember to turn it off when you're back on the ground.

If you plug the iPhone into an iPod accessory that isn't necessarily compatible because of possible interference from the iPhone's wireless radios, it offers to turn on airplane mode for you, as the message displayed in Figure 13-2 indicates.

Figure 13-2: Saying yes to this message may eliminate the static.

Wi-Fi

As previously discussed, Wi-Fi is one of the two wireless networks you can use to surf the Web, send e-mail, and so on. It's faster than AT&T's EDGE data network, your other path to the Internet on the iPhone.

You use the Wi-Fi setting to determine which Wi-Fi networks are available to you and which one to exploit based on its signal.

Tap Wi-Fi and all Wi-Fi networks in range are displayed, as shown in Figure 13-3. (Alternatively, you can reach this screen by tapping the General setting, tapping Network, and then tapping Wi-Fi.)

A signal strength indicator can help you choose the network to connect to if more than one is listed; tap the appropriate Wi-Fi network when you've reached a decision. If a network is password-protected, you'll see a lock icon.

You can also turn the Ask to Join Networks setting on or off. Networks that the iPhone is already familiar with are joined automatically regardless of which you choose. If the Ask feature is on, you are asked before joining a new network. If off, you have to manually select a network.

If you no longer want the iPhone to join a particular network you've used before automatically, tap the > symbol next to the network in question within Wi-Fi settings and then tap Forget This Network. The iPhone develops a quick case of amnesia.

In some instances you have to supply other technical information about a network you hope to glom onto. You'll encounter a bunch of nasty sounding terms: DHCP, Boot IP, Static, IP Address, Subnet Mask, Router, DNS, Search Domains, Client ID, and HTTP Proxy. Chances are that none of this info is at the tip of your tongue, and that's okay. For one thing, most of you will never need to know this stuff. What's more, even if you do have to fill in or adjust these settings, a network administrator or techie friend can probably help you out.

Figure 13-3: Checking out your Wi-Fi options.

Sometimes you may want to connect to a network that is closed and not shown on the Wi-Fi list. If so, tap Other and use the keyboard to enter the network name. Then tap to choose the type of security setting the network is using (if any). Your choices are WEP Password, WEP hex or ASCII, WPA, and WPA2. Again, not exactly the friendliest terminology, but we hope someone nearby can provide assistance.

If no Wi-Fi network is available, you have to rely on EDGE. If that's not available either, you won't be able rocket into cyberspace until you regain access to a network.

Using Usage

Think of the Usage setting as one of the places to go on the iPhone for statistics on how you actually employ the device. It's not the only place to tap the Settings screen for user stats; you get other information in the About setting (under General on the Settings screen), described later in this chapter.

You can scroll up or down the Usage list to discover the following:

- **The amount of time since you last fully charged your iPhone:** This is indicated in days and hours, both for the time when the iPhone has been unlocked and used and when it's been locked and in standby mode.
- **Call time:** Shown for the current period and the lifetime of the product.
- **EDGE stats:** The amount of network data you've sent and received over EDGE. You can reset these statistics by tapping the Reset Statistics button at the bottom of the screen.

Settings for Your Senses

The next set of settings have to do with what the iPhone looks like and sounds like.

Sounds

Consider Sounds the iPhone's sound stage. Here's where you can turn audio alerts on or off for a variety of functions: new voicemails, new text messages, new mail, sent mail, and calendar alerts. This is also where you set ringtones (as described in Chapter 4).

Other options: You can decide whether you want to hear lock sounds and keyboard clicks. You can determine whether the iPhone should vibrate when you get a call. And you can drag the volume slider to determine how loud your ringer and alerts will be.

There is an alternative: You can also use the physical Volume buttons on the side of the iPhone for this purpose, provided you're not already on a call or using the iPod to listen to music or watch video.

Brightening up your day

Who doesn't want a bright vibrant screen? Alas, the brightest screens exact a tradeoff. Before you drag the brightness slider shown in Figure 13-4 to the max, remember that brighter screens sap the life out of your battery more quickly.

That's why we recommend tapping the Auto-Brightness control so that it is On. It adjusts the screen according to the lighting conditions around the iPhone while being considerate to your battery.

Wallpaper

Choosing wallpaper is a neat way to dress up the iPhone according to your taste. You can sample the pretty patterns and designs that the iPhone has already chosen for you by tapping the thumbnails shown in Figure 13-5. Of course, although the Mona Lisa is one of your choices, DaVinci has nothing over the masterpieces in your own photo albums (as described in Chapter 9). After making a selection, tap the image and then tap Set Wallpaper.

Figure 13-4: Sliding this control adjusts screen brightness.

Figure 13-5: Choosing a masterpiece background.

In General

Certain miscellaneous settings are difficult to pigeonhole. Apple wisely lumped these under the General settings moniker. Let's take a look.

About About

You are not seeing double. This section is all about the setting known as About. And About is full of trivial and not-so-trivial information about the device. What you'll find here:

- Name of your network.

- Number of songs stored on the device.

- Number of videos.

- Number of photos.

- Storage capacity used and available. Because of the way the device is formatted, you'll always have a little less storage than the 4 or 8 gigabytes of flash memory advertised.

- Software version. You probably think you own version 1.0 of the iPhone, and in fact that's so. But as the software gets tweaked and updated, your device goes a little beyond that 1.0 starting point. So in parentheses next to the version number, you'll see something like 1A543a. That (or another string of numbers and letters) is the build number of the software version you have. It changes when the iPhone's software is updated.

- Serial and model numbers.

- Wi-Fi address.

- Bluetooth address. More on Bluetooth shortly.

- IMEI and ICCID. Say what? These stand for the International Mobile Equipment Identity and Integrated Circuit Card Identifier (or Smart Card) numbers. Hey, we warned you some of this was trivial.

- Modern firmware. The version of the cellular transmitter.

- Legal. You had to know that the lawyers would get their two cents in somehow. All the fine print is here. And *fine print* it is. Although you can flick to scroll through these lengthy legal notices, you can't pinch the screen to enlarge the text. Not that we can imagine more than a handful of you will bother to read this legal mumbo-jumbo.

Date and time

In our neck of the woods, the time is reported as 11:32 PM or whatever time it happens to be. But in some circles, it's reported as 23:32. If you prefer the latter format on the iPhone's status bar, tap the 24-Hour Time setting (under Date & Time) so that it is On.

This is just one of the settings you can adjust under Date & Time. You can also have the iPhone set the time automatically using the time reported by the cellular network (and adjusted for the time zone you are in).

If turned off, you'll be asked to choose the time zone and set the date and time. Here's how:

1. **Tap Set Automatically so that it is Off.**

   You see fields for setting the time zone and the date and time.

2. **Tap the Time Zone field so that the current time zone and virtual keyboard are shown.**

3. **Tap out the letters of the city or country whose time zone you want to enter until the one you have in mind appears. Then tap the name of that city or country.**

   The Time Zone is automatically filled in for that city.

4. **Tap the Set Date & Time field so that the time is shown. Then roll the bicycle lock–like controls until the proper time is displayed.**

5. **Tap the date shown so that the bicycle lock–like controls pop up for the date. Then roll the wheels for the month, day, and year until the correct date appears.**

6. **Tap the Date & Time button to return to main Date & Time settings screen.**

The last set of date and time controls concern your calendar. You get to choose whether to turn the Time Zone Support feature on or off. If on, the events in your calendar are displayed according to the time zone you selected for your calendar. If off, those entries are displayed according to your current whereabouts.

Auto-lock

You can set the amount of time before the phone automatically locks or turns off the display. Your choices are five minutes before, four minutes before, and so on all the way down to one minute. Or you can set it so that the iPhone never locks automatically.

Don't worry if the iPhone is locked. You can still get calls and text messages and adjust the volume.

Passcode

You can choose a passcode to prevent people from unlocking the phone. Tap Passcode Lock. Then use the virtual keypad to enter a 4-digit code. During this setup, you have to enter the code a second time before it is accepted.

You can change the passcode or turn it off later, but you need to know the present passcode to apply any changes. If you forget the passcode, you have to restore the iPhone's software, as described in the next chapter.

FYI on VPN

A *virtual private network,* or VPN, is a way for you to securely access your company's network behind the firewall. The iPhone supports some VPN protocol configurations (pretty much the same ones as those on the Mac) and we're about to tell you their names, not that they'll mean much to anyone lacking network administration or IT credentials.

Here goes: The iPhone supports protocols known as *L2TP* (layer 2 tunneling protocol) and *PPTP* (point-to-point tunneling protocol).

You get to these by tapping General, Network, VPN, and then Settings. Then using configuration settings provided by your company, fill in the appropriate server information, account, password, encryption level (if appropriate), and so on. Better yet, lend your iPhone to the techies at the place you work and let them fill in the blanks on your behalf.

Once configured, you can turn VPN on or off by tapping the VPN On or Off switch inside Settings.

Brushing up on Bluetooth

Of all the peculiar terms you may encounter in techdom, *Bluetooth* is one of our favorites. The name is derived from a tenth-century Viking king named Harald Blatand, who, the story goes, helped unite warring factions. (And Bluetooth is all about collaboration between different types of devices, get it?) We're told Blatand translates to Bluetooth in English.

Blatand was obviously ahead of his time, though we can't imagine he ever dialed a cell phone. But today he has an entire short-range wireless technology named in his honor. On the iPhone, you can use Bluetooth to communicate wirelessly with a compatible Bluetooth headset or hands-free car kit. Such optional headsets and kits are made by Apple and others.

To ensure that the iPhone works with one of these devices, they have to be coupled, or paired. With the optional iPhone Bluetooth headset that Apple sells, you can automatically pair the devices by placing the iPhone and headset into a dual dock (supplied with the headset), which you connect to your computer.

If you're using a third-party accessory, follow the instructions that came with that headset or car kit so that it becomes *discoverable,* or ready to be paired with your iPhone Then turn on Bluetooth under General on the Settings screen so that the iPhone can find such nearby devices, and the device can find the iPhone. Bluetooth works up to a range of about 30 feet.

You'll know Bluetooth is turned on when you see the Bluetooth icon in the status bar. If the symbol is blue or black, the iPhone is communicating wirelessly with a connected device. If it is gray, Bluetooth is turned on in the iPhone but a paired device is not nearby or on.

To unpair a device, select it from the device list shown in Figure 13-6 and tap Unpair.

As of this writing, Bluetooth on the iPhone was limited compared to the Bluetooth capabilities of some other devices. It does not work with *stereo* Bluetooth headsets. You can't use Bluetooth to exchange files or sync with a computer wirelessly. Nor can you use it to print stuff from the iPhone through a Bluetooth printer. That's because the iPhone does not support any of the Bluetooth *profiles* required to allow such wireless stunts to take place.

Figure 13-6: Falling out of love. Unpairing devices.

Keyboard

You can do two main things under Keyboard settings. You can turn Auto-Capitalization on or off and turn Enable Caps Lock on or off.

Auto-capitalization, which the iPhone turns on by default, means that the first letter of the first word you type after ending a previous sentence with a period, question mark, or exclamation point will be capitalized.

If Cap Locks is enabled, all letters will be uppercased LIKE THIS if you double-tap the shift key. The shift key is the one with the arrow pointing north.

Reset

As little kids playing sports, we'd end an argument by agreeing to a "do-over." Well the Reset settings on the iPhone are one big do-over. Now that we're (presumably) grown up, think long and hard about the consequences before implementing do-over settings. That said, you may encounter good reasons for starting over; some of these are addressed in the troubleshooting chapter following this one.

Here are your reset options:

- **Reset All Settings:** Tapping here resets all settings, but no data or media is deleted.

- **Erase All Content and Settings:** This resets all settings *and* wipes out all your data.

- **Reset Dictionary:** As we pointed out early on, the iPhone's keyboard is intelligent. And part of the reason it's so smart is that it learns from you. So when you reject words that the iPhone keyboard suggests, it figures the words you specifically banged out ought to be added to the keyboard dictionary. Tapping Reset here removes those added words from the dictionary.

- **Reset Network Settings:** This deletes the current network settings and restores them to their factory defaults.

Phoning In More Settings

We've already covered most of the remaining settings in previous chapters devoted to the iPod (photos and music), Safari, and e-mail.

But way back in Chapter 4, we tipped our hand and indicated that we'd save a few more phone tricks — those found in Phone settings — for this chapter.

So tap Phone now to review some of the choices we didn't get to previously. Be aware you'll have to scroll down the screen to find Phone settings.

Sorting and displaying contacts

Do you think of us as Ed and Bob or Baig and LeVitus? The answer to that question will probably determine whether you choose to sort your Contacts list alphabetically by last name or first.

Tap Sort Contacts, and then tap either Last, First or First, Last. Tap the Phone button to return to the main Phone settings screen.

You can also determine whether you want to display a first name or last name first. Tap Display Contacts and then choose First, Last or Last, First. Tap the phone button when you are finished.

Call forwarding

If you expect to spend time in an area with poor cell phone coverage or none at all, you may want to temporarily forward calls to a landline or other portable handset. Here are the simple steps:

1. **On the Settings screen, tap Phone and then tap Call Forwarding.**

2. **Tap to turn on Call Forwarding.**

3. **Use the virtual keypad to enter the number where you want incoming calls to ring.**

4. **Tap the Call Forwarding button to return to the main Call Forwarding screen.**

To change the forwarding number, tap the circle with the x in the phone number field to get rid of the old number, and then enter a new one.

Remember to turn off Call Forwarding to receive calls directly on your iPhone again.

You must have cellular coverage while setting the call forwarding feature.

Call waiting

Tap the Call Waiting button to turn the feature on or off. If Call Waiting is off and you are speaking on the phone, the call is automatically dispatched to voicemail.

Displaying Caller ID

Don't want your name or number displayed on the phone you are calling? Make sure to tap Show My Caller ID so it is Off. If privacy isn't a concern, you can leave this setting On.

TTY

Folks who are hearing impaired sometimes rely on a teletype, or TTY machine, to hold conversations. You can use the iPhone with standard TTY devices by plugging a cable from the TTY device to an optional $19 iPhone TTY adapter and then plugging the adapter into the iPhone. Make sure the TTY setting on the phone is turned On.

Locking your SIM

The tiny SIM (Subscriber Identity Module) card inside your iPhone holds your phone number and other important data. Tap to turn on SIM PIN and enter a password with the keypad. That way, if someone gets hold of your SIM, he or she can't use it in another phone without the password. Be aware that if you assign a PIN to your SIM, you have to enter it to turn the iPhone off and on again.

AT&T Services

There's a major difference between the iPhone and all the other Apple products you might buy. That's because you are entering into a relationship not only with Apple but also with the phone company. Tap AT&T Services and then tap any of the following for a shortcut phone call to

- ✓ **Check Bill Balance:** The phone dials *225# and, if all goes according to plan, you receive a text message with the due date and sum owed, as shown in Figure 13-7. Such text messages are not counted against your messaging allotment.

- **Call Directory Assistance:** The phone dials 411.

- **Pay My Bill:** The iPhone dials *729 and you are connected to an automated voice system. You can pay your bill with a checking account, debit card, or credit card by following the voice prompts.

It's important to note that you are billed for phone service from AT&T, not Apple. Of course any music or other content purchased in iTunes from your computer is paid to Apple, as with any iPod.

- **View My Minutes:** This time *646# is called. You again receive a text reply that doesn't count against your messaging allotment.

- **Voice Connect:** The iPhone dials *08 to connect you to automated news, weather, sports, quotes, and more. Just bark out the kind of information you're looking for, such as "finance," and follow voice prompts for stock quotes, business news, and so on. Or say "sports" and follow voice prompts to get the latest scores from your favorite team.

Figure 13-7: You can check your phone bill via a text message.

Not all AT&T Services make a phone call. If you tap the AT&T MyAccount button, Safari opens an AT&T account management page on the Web.

We trust that you control freaks are satisfied with all the stuff you can manage inside Settings. Still, the iPhone may not always behave as you want. For the times when things get *out* of control, we highly recommend the next chapter.

When Good iPhones Go Bad

*I*n our experience, iPhones are usually reliable devices. And most users we've talked to have reported trouble-free operation. Notice our use of the word *most.* That's because every so often, a good iPhone goes bad — but it's not a common occurrence. So in this chapter we look at all the types of bad things that can happen: problems with the phone itself; problems making or receiving calls; issues with wireless networks; and trouble with synchronization, computers (both Mac and PC), or iTunes.

After all the troubleshooting, we tell you how to get even more help if nothing we've suggested does the trick. And finally, if your iPhone is so badly hosed that it needs to go back to the mothership for repairs, we offer ways to survive the experience with a minimum of stress or fuss.

©iStockphoto.com/Jonathan Maddock

iPhone Issues

Our first category of troubleshooting techniques applies to an iPhone that is frozen or otherwise acting up. The recommended procedure when this happens is to perform the six *R*'s in sequence. What are the six R's? Glad you asked. They are

↙ Recharge

↙ Restart

  ✐ Reset your iPhone

  ✐ Remove your content

  ✐ Reset settings and content

  ✐ Restore

So if your iPhone acts up on you — if it freezes, won't wake up from sleep, won't do something it used to do, or in any other way acts improperly — this section describes the things you should try in the order we (and Apple) recommend you try them.

If the first technique doesn't do the trick, go on to the second. If the second one doesn't work, try the third. And so on.

Recharge

If your iPhone acts up in any way, shape, or form, the first thing you should try is to give its battery a full recharge.

Don't plug the iPhone's dock connector–to–USB cable into a USB port on your keyboard, monitor, or USB hub. You need to plug it into one of the USB ports on your computer itself because USB ports on your computer supply more power than the other ports.

You can use the included USB power adapter to recharge your iPhone from an AC outlet rather than from a computer.

Restart

If you recharge your iPhone and it still misbehaves, the next thing to try is restarting it. Just as restarting a computer often fixes problems, restarting your iPhone sometimes works wonders.

To do so:

  1. **Press and hold the Sleep/Wake button.**

  2. **Slide the red slider to turn the iPhone off, and then wait a few seconds.**

  3. **Press and hold the Sleep/Wake button again until the Apple logo appears on the screen.**

  4. **If your iPod is still frozen, misbehaves, or doesn't start, press and hold the Home button for 6 to 10 seconds to force any frozen applications to quit, and then perform Steps 1 to 3 again.**

If this doesn't get your iPhone back up and running, move on to the third *R*, resetting your iPhone.

Reset your iPhone

To reset your iPhone, merely press and hold the Sleep/Wake button while you press the Home button on the front. When you see the Apple logo, release both buttons.

Resetting your iPhone is like forcing your computer to restart after a crash. Your data shouldn't be affected by a reset and in many cases it will cure whatever was ailing your iPhone. So don't be shy about giving this technique a try. In many cases, your iPhone will be back to normal after you've reset it this way.

Unfortunately, sometimes resetting *doesn't* do the trick. When that's the case, you have to take stronger measures.

Remove content

Up to now, nothing you've done should have taken more than a minute or two. We hate to tell you, but this is about to change. Because the next thing you should try is removing some or all of your data to see whether perhaps it's the cause of your troubles.

To do so, you'll need to sync your iPhone and reconfigure it so that some or all of your files are not synchronized (which will remove them from the phone). The problem could be contacts, calendar data, songs, photos, videos, or podcasts. If you suspect a particular data type — for example, you suspect your photos because whenever you tap the Photos icon on the Home screen your iPhone freezes — try removing that data first.

Or, if you have no suspicions, uncheck every item and sync. When you're finished your iPhone should have no data on it.

If that fixed it, try restoring your data one type at a time. If the problem returns, you have to keep experimenting to determine which particular data type or file is causing the problem.

If you're still having problems, the next step is to reset your iPhone's settings.

Reset settings and content

This is actually two steps: The first one, resetting your iPhone settings, resets every iPhone setting to its default — the way it was when you took it out of the box. Resetting the iPhone's settings doesn't erase any of your data or media. The only downside is that you may have to go back and change some settings afterwards. So this is a step you can try without trepidation. To do it, tap the Settings icon on your Home screen, and then tap General, Reset, and Reset All Settings.

Be careful *not* to tap Erase All Content and Settings, at least not yet. Erasing all content takes more time to recover from (because your next sync takes a long time), so you should try Reset All Settings first.

Now, if resetting all settings didn't cure your iPhone, you have to try Erase All Content and Settings. You'll find it in the same place as Reset All Settings (tap Settings, General, Reset).

This will delete everything from your iPhone — all of your data, media, and settings. Because all of these things are stored on your computer, at least in theory, you should be able to put things back the way they were with your next sync. But you will lose any photos you've taken, as well as contacts, calendar events, and On-the-Go playlists you've created or modified since your last sync.

After using Erase All Content and Settings, check to see whether your iPhone works properly. If it doesn't cure what ails your iPhone, the final *R* is restoring your iPhone using iTunes.

Restore

Before you give up the ghost on your poor, sick iPhone, you can try one more thing. Connect your iPhone to your computer as though you were about to sync. But when the iPhone appears in the iTunes source list, click the Restore button on the Summary tab. This will erase all of your data and media, and reset all of your settings as well.

Because all of your data and media still exists on your computer (except photos you've taken, and contacts, calendar events, and On-the-Go playlists you've created or modified since your last sync, as noted previously), you shouldn't lose anything by restoring. Your next sync will take longer than usual, and you may have to reset settings you've changed since you got your iPhone. But other than those inconveniences, restoring shouldn't cause you any additional trouble.

Okay. So that's the gamut of things you can do when your iPhone acts up. If none of this worked, skim through the rest of the chapter to see whether anything else we recommend looks like it might help. If not, your iPhone probably needs to go into the shop for repairs.

Never fear, gentle reader. Be sure and read the last section in this chapter, "If Nothing We Suggested Worked." Your iPhone may be very sick, but we'll help ease the pain by sharing some tips on how to minimize the discomfort.

Problems with Calling or Networks

If you're having problems making or receiving calls, problems sending or receiving SMS text messages, or problems with Wi-Fi or AT&T's EDGE data network, this section may help. The techniques here are short and sweet — except for the last one, restore. Restore, which we described in the previous section, is still inconvenient and time consuming, and it still entails erasing all of your data and media and then restoring it.

But first, here are some simple steps that may help. Once again, we suggest you try them in this order (and so does Apple).

1. **Check the cell signal icon in the top-left corner of the screen.**

   If you don't have at least one or two bars, you may not be able to use the phone or SMS text message function.

2. **Make sure you haven't left your iPhone in airplane mode, as described in the Chapter 13.**

   In airplane mode, all network-dependent features are disabled, so you can't make or receive phone calls, send or receive SMS text messages, or use any of the applications that require a Wi-Fi or EDGE network connection (that is, Mail, Safari, Stocks, Maps, and Weather).

3. **Try moving around.**

   Changing your location by as little as a few feet can sometimes mean the difference between four bars and zero bars, or being able to use the EDGE data network or not. If you're inside, try going outside. If you're outside, try moving ten or twenty paces in any direction. Keep an eye on the cell signal icon as you move around and stop when you see more bars than you saw before.

4. **Turn airplane mode on by tapping Settings on the Home screen and then tapping the Airplane Mode On/Off switch to turn it on. Wait 15 or 20 seconds and then turn it off again.**

Toggling airplane mode on and off like this resets both the Wi-Fi and EDGE wireless connections. So if your network connection was the problem, toggling airplane mode on and off may very well correct it.

5. **Restart your iPhone.**

If you've forgotten how, refer to the "Restart" section a few pages back. As we mentioned, restarting your iPhone is often all it takes to fix whatever was wrong.

6. **Make sure your SIM card is firmly seated.**

A SIM (Subscriber Identity Module) card is a removable smart card used to identify mobile phones. It allows users to change phones by moving the SIM card from one phone to another.

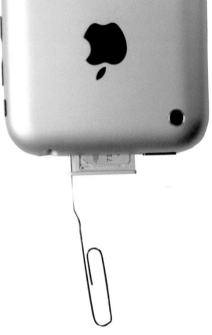

To remove the SIM card, find a very fine gauge paper clip, straighten one end, and then stick the straight end gently into the hole on the SIM tray, as shown in Figure 14-1.

Figure 14-1: Removing the SIM tray.

When the SIM tray slides out, carefully lift out the SIM card and then reinsert it, making sure it's firmly situated in the tray before you gently push the tray back in until it locks.

If none of the preceding fixed your network issues, try restoring your iPhone as described previously in the "Restore" section.

Performing a restore deletes everything on your iPhone — all of your data, media, and settings. You should be able to put things back the way they were with your next sync. If that doesn't happen for whatever reason, you can't say we didn't warn you.

Sync, Computer, or iTunes Issues

Our last category of troubleshooting techniques applies to issues that involve synchronization and computer/iPhone relations. If you're having problems syncing or your computer doesn't recognize your iPhone when you connect it, here are some things to try.

Once again we suggest that you try these procedures in the order they're presented here.

1. **Recharge your iPhone.**

   If you didn't try it previously, try it now. Go back to the "iPhone Issues" section at the beginning of the chapter and read what we said about recharging your iPhone. Every word there also applies here.

2. **Try a different USB port or a different cable if you have one available.**

   It doesn't happen often, but occasionally USB ports and cables go bad. When they do, it invariably causes sync and connection problems. So it's always a good idea to make sure that a bad USB port or cable isn't to blame.

   If you don't remember what we've said about using USB ports on your computer rather than the ones on your keyboard, monitor, or hub, we suggest you reread the "Recharge" section, earlier in the chapter.

3. **Restart your iPhone and try to sync again.**

   We describe restarting in full and loving detail in the "Restart" section, earlier in the chapter.

4. **Reinstall iTunes.**

   Even if you have an iTunes installer handy, it's probably a good idea to visit the Apple Web site and download the latest and greatest version, just in case. You'll always find the latest version of iTunes at `www.apple.com/itunes/download/`.

More Help on the Apple Web Site

If you've tried everything suggested so far and are still having problems, don't give up just yet. Here are a few more places you may find help. We recommend that you check out some or all of them before you throw in the towel and smash your iPhone into tiny little pieces (or ship it back to Apple for repairs, as described in the next section).

First, Apple offers an excellent set of support resources on its Web site at `www.apple.com/support/iphone`. You can browse support issues by category, search for a problem by keyword, or use the iPhone Troubleshooting Assistant to resolve common problems, as shown in Figure 14-2.

TIP

We wouldn't put a lot of hope in the Troubleshooting Assistant. If you've tried everything we've suggested in this chapter, you've probably tried everything the Troubleshooting Assistant will suggest. However, since it's easier to update a Web site than it is to update a book, the Troubleshooting Assistant could offer techniques we didn't know when we wrote this. So although it may just repeat things you already know, it could also have something new. Give it a try.

Figure 14-2: Apple's iPhone support pages offer several kinds of helpful information.

While you're visiting the Apple support pages, another section could be helpful: the discussion forums. You'll find them at `http://discussions.apple.com`, and they're chock full of questions and answers from other iPhone users. It's been our experience that if you can't find an answer to a support question elsewhere, you can often find something helpful in these forums. You can browse by category, as shown in Figure 14-3, or search by keyword.

Either way, you'll find thousands of discussions about almost every aspect of using your iPhone. Better still, you'll frequently find the answer to your question or a helpful suggestion, as shown in Figure 14-4.

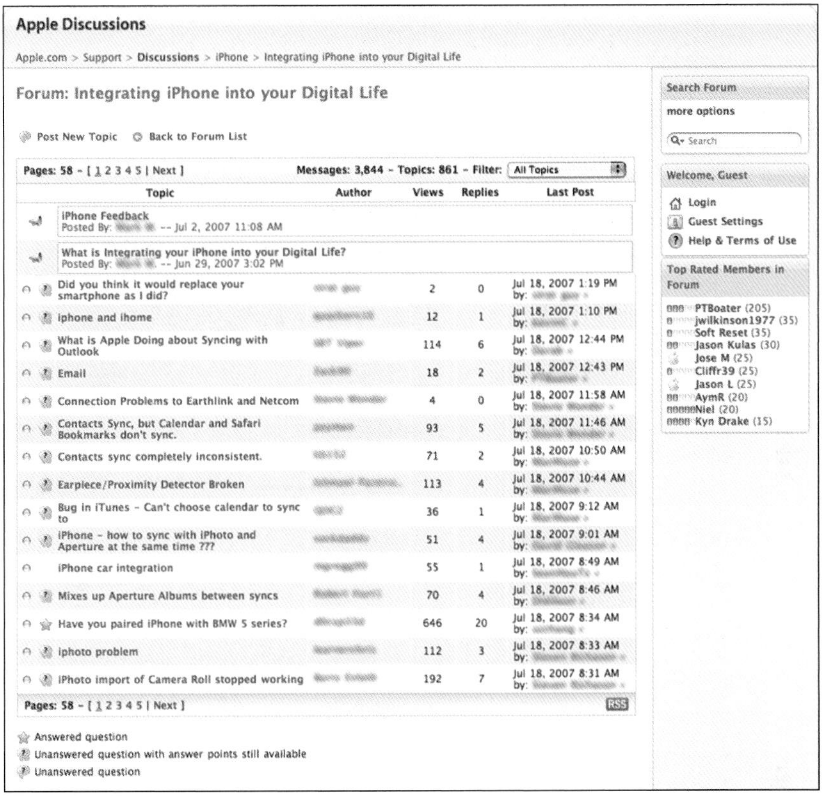

Figure 14-3: Page 1 of 58 pages of discussions about integrating the iPhone into your digital life.

Now for the best part. If you can't find a solution by browsing or searching, you can post your question in the appropriate Apple discussion forum. Check back in a few days (or even a few hours) and some helpful iPhone user may very well have replied with the answer. If you've never tried this fabulous tool, you're missing out on one of the greatest support resources available anywhere.

Last, but certainly not least, before you give up the ghost you might want to try a carefully worded Google search. It couldn't hurt and you might just find the solution you've spent hours searching for.

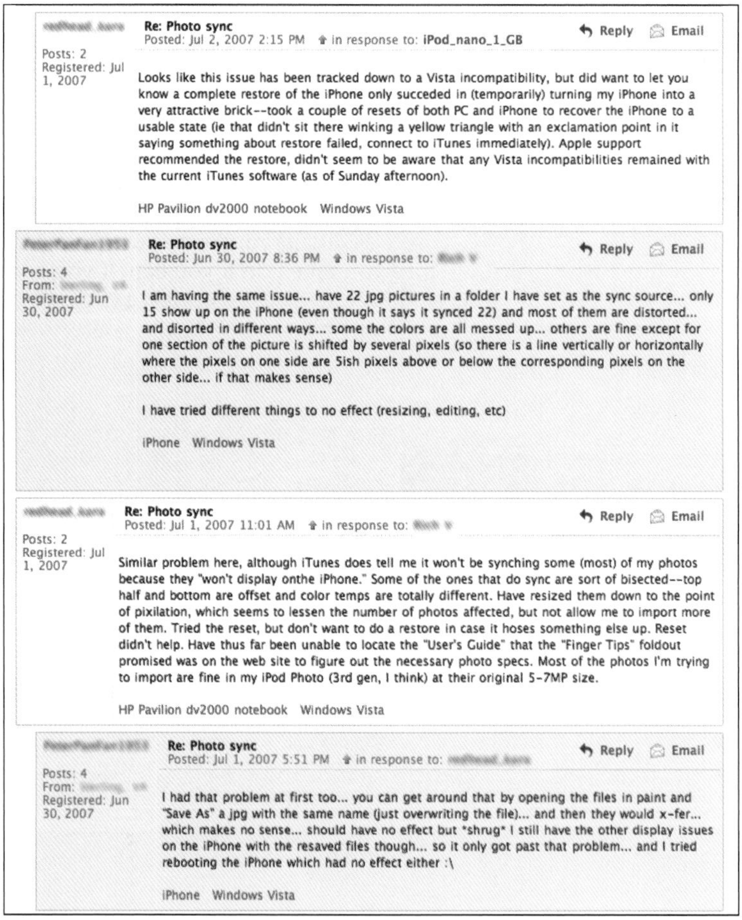

Re: Photo sync
Posted: Jul 2, 2007 2:15 PM   ↟ in response to: iPod_nano_1_GB   ↩ Reply   ✉ Email

Posts: 2
Registered: Jul 1, 2007

Looks like this issue has been tracked down to a Vista incompatibility, but did want to let you know a complete restore of the iPhone only succeded in (temporarily) turning my iPhone into a very attractive brick--took a couple of resets of both PC and iPhone to recover the iPhone to a usable state (ie that didn't sit there winking a yellow triangle with an exclamation point in it saying something about restore failed, connect to iTunes immediately). Apple support recommended the restore, didn't seem to be aware that any Vista incompatibilities remained with the current iTunes software (as of Sunday afternoon).

HP Pavilion dv2000 notebook   Windows Vista

Re: Photo sync
Posted: Jun 30, 2007 8:36 PM   ↟ in response to: ███ ▓   ↩ Reply   ✉ Email

Posts: 4
From: ███, ██
Registered: Jun 30, 2007

I am having the same issue... have 22 jpg pictures in a folder I have set as the sync source... only 15 show up on the iPhone (even though it says it synced 22) and most of them are distorted... and disorted in different ways... some the colors are all messed up... others are fine except for one section of the picture is shifted by several pixels (so there is a line vertically or horizontally where the pixels on one side are 5ish pixels above or below the corresponding pixels on the other side... if that makes sense)

I have tried different things to no effect (resizing, editing, etc)

iPhone   Windows Vista

Re: Photo sync
Posted: Jul 1, 2007 11:01 AM   ↟ in response to: ███ ▓   ↩ Reply   ✉ Email

Posts: 2
Registered: Jul 1, 2007

Similar problem here, although iTunes does tell me it won't be synching some (most) of my photos because they "won't display onthe iPhone." Some of the ones that do sync are sort of bisected--top half and bottom are offset and color temps are totally different. Have resized them down to the point of pixilation, which seems to lessen the number of photos affected, but not allow me to import more of them. Tried the reset, but don't want to do a restore in case it hoses something else up. Reset didn't help. Have thus far been unable to locate the "User's Guide" that the "Finger Tips" foldout promised was on the web site to figure out the necessary photo specs. Most of the photos I'm trying to import are fine in my iPod Photo (3rd gen, I think) at their original 5-7MP size.

HP Pavilion dv2000 notebook   Windows Vista

Re: Photo sync
Posted: Jul 1, 2007 5:51 PM   ↟ in response to: ███ ███   ↩ Reply   ✉ Email

Posts: 4
From: ███, ██
Registered: Jun 30, 2007

I had that problem at first too... you can get around that by opening the files in paint and "Save As" a jpg with the same name (just overwriting the file)... and then they would x~fer... which makes no sense... should have no effect but *shrug* I still have the other display issues on the iPhone with the resaved files though... so it only got past that problem... and I tried rebooting the iPhone which had no effect either :\

iPhone   Windows Vista

Figure 14-4: A typical discussion in an iPhone discussion forum.

If Nothing We Suggested So Far Helped

If you've tried every trick in the book (this one) and still have a malfunctioning iPhone, it's time to consider shipping it off to the iPhone hospital (better known as Apple, Inc.). The repair will be free if your iPhone is still under its one-year limited warranty.

You can extend your warranty to up to two years from the original purchase date if you want. To do so, you need to buy the AppleCare Protection Plan for your iPhone. You don't have to do it when you buy the phone, but you must buy it before your one-year limited warranty expires. The cost is $69.

Here are a few things you should know before you take your phone in to be repaired:

 ✒ Your iPhone will be erased during its repair, so you should sync your iPhone with iTunes before you take it in if you can. If you can't and you've entered data on the phone since your last sync, such as a contact or an appointment, the data won't be there when you restore your iPhone upon its return.

 ✒ Remove any third-party accessories such as a case or screen protector.

 ✒ Remove the SIM card from your iPhone (as described in the "Problems with Calling or Networks" section) and keep it in a safe place.

Do not under any circumstances forget this step. Apple will not guarantee that your SIM card will be returned to you after a repair. If you do forget this step, Apple suggests that you contact your local AT&T store and obtain a new SIM card with the proper account information. Ouch.

Although you may be able to get your iPhone serviced by AT&T or by mail, we recommend that you take it to your nearest Apple Store for two reasons:

 ✒ No one knows your iPhone like Apple. One of the geniuses at the Apple Store may be able to fix whatever is wrong without sending your iPhone away for repairs.

 ✒ Only the Apple Store offers a loaner phone while yours is in for repairs. It's called the AppleCare Service Phone, and you can use one until your iPhone comes back for just $29.

If you choose to borrow an AppleCare Service Phone, there's no activation required and the loaner will have the same phone number as the phone that's in the shop. Just pop your SIM card into the loaner and away you go.

You can sync your AppleCare Service Phone with iTunes on your computer to fill it with the data and media files you had on your sick iPhone. When you get your iPhone back after repairs, just reverse the process. Pop the SIM card into it and sync it with iTunes on your computer and you're good to go.

Part VI
The Part of Tens

*I*t's written in stone somewhere at Wiley world headquarters that we Dummies authors must include a Part of Tens in every single Dummies book we write. It is a duty we take quite seriously. So in this part, you find our wish list — all the things we wish the iPhone had that it doesn't (yet), from being able to tap into a speedier cell phone network to offering a swappable battery. Because as infatuated as we are with the iPhone, we are obliged to point out that it is less than perfect.

We then move on to our diverse collection of ten fabulous Web resources every iPhone user should know about. We tell you about online destinations to practice typing on iPhone's multitouch display, calculate tips, and compile a shopping list. Even your very fortune awaits you in these next few pages.

We close the show with one of our favorite topics: hints, tips, and shortcuts that make life with your iPhone even better. Among the ten, you discover how to look at the capacity of your newly-favored device in different ways, find out how to share Web pages, and pick up another trick or two on using iPhone's virtual keyboard. (Ten points if you can guess what these three photos have in common.)

15

Ten Things for the Wish List

nquestionably, Apple deserves high praise for the iPhone. It's a fabulous device that breaks new ground and will likely spur innovation in the entire cell phone industry. We think that's terrific.

But we wouldn't be doing our jobs as journalists if we didn't point out shortcomings. As smitten as we are over what is really a handheld computer more than a cell phone, the fact is version 1.0 of the iPhone isn't flawless. Some features that we would have wanted to see were left out, while others could simply perform better.

In that spirit, we submit ten items for an iPhone wish list. The good news is that Apple can beef up certain features and correct bugs through software upgrades. For example, Apple could upgrade the iPhone so that it can support Flash video, among other Internet standards.

©iStockphoto.com/Paul Cowan

It's possible that by the time you read this chapter, Apple or AT&T will have addressed some of the things on our list.

But not all. So while we're certainly not advising you to hold off buying an iPhone if you haven't purchased one yet, the truth is you won't be punished by waiting. The next iteration of the iPhone, and the one after that — whenever Apple gets around to introducing new models — will almost certainly be better than their predecessors. Quite possibly cheaper too.

Hey, this is a chapter for wishful thinkers.

A Faster Network

If critics have consistently taken Apple to task on anything iPhone-related, it is the too-often plodding EDGE data network run by partner AT&T. In Chapter 10, we describe how EDGE is not quite a true 3G, or third-generation, data network.

AT&T is already working with faster networks than EDGE, even if those are not nearly as ubiquitous today. They are based on technologies known as *UMTS* (Universal Mobile Telephone System) and *HSDPA* (High-Speed Downlink Packet Access). Although AT&T claims typical speeds for EDGE of 75 to 135 kilobits per second, UMTS can deliver 220 to 320 kbps and HSDPA, 400 to 700 kbps. That puts the networks in the same ballpark as the broadband Internet service you may be experiencing at home through a cable modem or DSL.

We can't predict when the AT&T and Apple union will lead to a true 3G iPhone. There are lingering issues. For one, too few potential customers have access to these faster networks at the moment.

And Steve Jobs himself, while wishing for faster service, told the *Wall Street Journal* that the early 3G chipsets were not "low-enough power" (affecting battery life) and "took up too much physical space."

In the meantime, there's always Wi-Fi, if you happen to have access to a network.

Freedom of Choice

You are currently limited to using an iPhone with AT&T in the U.S., O2 in the U.K., T-Mobile in Germany, and Orange in France. If you'd rather give your business to another wireless carrier — well, you're out of luck.

Now we have nothing against those four wireless operators per se. But when it comes to cell phone carriers, we are decidedly pro-choice. Other smart-phones are sold across multiple carriers. So why not the iPhone? We're already wondering out loud if the agreement between the companies has a loophole that would let Apple make iPhones available through other wireless phone companies. Only time will tell.

iTunes Ringtones and Music Downloads

It would seem like a natural: using snippets of music from your iTunes library for ringtones After all, one of the chief ways people personalize cell phones is through ringtones. And with iTunes you have this fabulous stash of music.

Not so fast.

There's no obvious technical reason stopping Apple from letting you pluck ringtones from your very own iTunes collection. But certain issues need to be resolved, such as the ever-sticky matter of digital rights and who owns what songs for what purpose. And pricing; it's astounding to us how much money is spent on ringtones.

While you can't convert songs in your iTunes Library into ringtones, you can create your own custom 30-second ringtones from certain songs you purchase from the iTunes Store (about 500,000 at this writing). Songs that can be made into ringtones are designated by a little "bell" symbol in iTunes; click the bell symbol to bring up iTunes' ringtone editor. Alas, each ringtone costs 99 cents, even if you've purchased the same song previously.

On a quasirelated topic, kudos to Apple for its recent introduction of the iTunes Wi-Fi Music Store, which lets you purchase and download music to your iPhone and then sync it with your PC or Mac later. That said, you can perform this magic only if you have access to a Wi-Fi network — it won't work when you're connected via the EDGE cellular data network. Furthermore, you can't buy video this way, only audio.

So we have three wishes:

1. **To create ringtones from our own songs without paying for them again.**
2. **To buy music over the EDGE cellular network.**
3. **To buy video content from our iPhones.**

Games

Whether you are surfing the Web, listening to music, watching videos, or composing e-mail, the iPhone gives you plenty of things to do while you're killing time commuting or waiting to board an airplane.

But the iPhone left out one diversion: the ability to play iPod games. Apple already sells a bunch of games in iTunes for video iPods. You can find Sudoku and Ms. Pac-Man to Tetris and Texas Hold 'em, most for $4.99 a pop. We don't see why these and other titles couldn't be made available for the iPhone.

In all fairness, we have to admit that we've found many enjoyable Web-based games to play on our iPhones, including the following:

- Diamenty: `http://diamenty.myiphone.pl/`
- Scenario Poker: `http://iphone.scenario.com/`
- Solitaire: `http://www.iphone-solitaire.com/`
- Brickshooter: `http://www.brickshooter.com/online/?iphone`

Although these online games may not be quite as polished as five dollar iPod games, they have a distinct advantage: They're all free.

The Ability to Use My Own Headphones

Not everyone likes the earbuds Apple supplies with its iPods and now the iPhone. Some folks have trouble keeping them in their ears. Some want richer sound. That's why a lot of people purchase their own headphones. But because of the way the headphone jack is recessed on the iPhone, not all of those third-party headphones can be plugged in.

You can already purchase inexpensive adapters that will let you plug in your headphones of choice. But some of these jut out awkwardly. We think an accessible jack that is compatible with all popular headphones ought to be standard on a future iPhone.

Of course, we're also in favor of dispensing with the wires altogether and letting you use state-of-the-art Bluetooth headphones instead. But the iPhone doesn't support Bluetooth stereo as of this writing.

A Built-in GPS

Don't get us wrong — the Maps application built into the iPhone rocks. But having experienced GPS-based navigation systems in our cars, we'd love to see a next-generation iPhone with a built-in GPS (Global Positioning System).

GPS would offer at least two big advantages over the current Maps app:

- You wouldn't need to know (or type) your current location. You'd open the Maps application and it would know where you are.
- Your iPhone would know what street you are on and be able to issue and update driving directions on-the-fly based on your current location.

Mobile devices with GPS are already available; it would be great to see it on the iPhone.

More Storage

Another thing we'd love to see are iPhones with more than the current maximum of 8GB of storage. It's not the end of the world having to pick and choose which audio, video, and photo files to sync with your 8GB iPhone, but it sure would be nice not to have to pick and choose at all.

For example, Bob's iPod video contains almost 30GB of music, podcasts, photos, and video. The size of Ed's iPod media collection is roughly the same. Nothing would be better than to have all of it available on our iPhones.

Who knows, maybe Apple will add a slot to a future iPhone for memory cards that would let you bolster storage capacities — or build an iPhone with a small hard drive.

Voice Dialing

Of all the things Apple left out of the iPhone, the lack of voice dialing puzzles us. Most mobile phones have it. Mac OS X has superb voice recognition software built into it. And unlike many mobile phones, the iPhone comes with a reasonably high-quality microphone. So we were surprised to find that we couldn't voice dial with the iPhone.

We're both big fans of wireless Bluetooth headsets and have enjoyed using them for voice dialing on our previous phones. Imagine you're driving and need to make a call. There's no doubt that pulling out your phone, looking at its screen, and choosing or dialing a number on it is dangerous — and possibly illegal. With voice dialing, you leave the phone in your pocket. To make a call, you just tap a button on your headset and say the person's name. A few seconds later, you're connected to that person.

We're going to go out on a limb and predict that Apple adds voice dialing before the end of 2007 via a software update to the iPhone. You heard it here first.

Removable Batteries

We both have iPhone battery rechargers in our homes, our offices, and our cars. Even so, there are times when it would be more convenient to slap in a fresh battery than hook the phone up to a power source for an hour or two.

Users would love it, and it would be another profitable accessory for Apple. We expect that someday the iPhone will include removable batteries. As far as we're concerned, the sooner the better.

A Video Camera

The lack of a video camera also puzzles us. Many mobile phones shoot video. Apple embeds a video camera in every notebook computer. And the iPhone is one of the best handheld devices for watching video. So why can't the camera built into the iPhone shoot video?

We know the video quality would be nothing to write home about, but we'd still love to shoot video with our iPhones.

Ten Terrific Web Resources

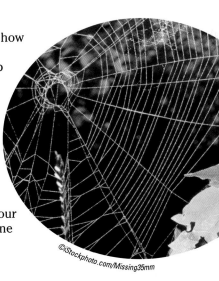

©iStockphoto.com/Missing35mm

All through this book you've heard us rave about how great the iPhone Internet experience is. But you can't have a great experience without some great Web sites to visit. And so here are ten Web sites that will make your iPhone even more useful or fun.

If you type faster on your computer than on your iPhone, bookmark these sites on your computer and then sync those bookmarks with your iPhone. And if you have more than a few iPhone-specific bookmarks, create an iPhone bookmark folder on your computer and put all of them into it. Then the next time you sync, that bookmark folder will appear on your iPhone, making it easy to use all of your favorite iPhone sites.

Wi-Fi Hotspot Finder Extraordinaire

Sure, you can use the Maps application to find a Wi-Fi hotspot in a pinch. Just tap Maps, then type *hotspot* and the zip code you want to search. Assuming that zip code has some Wi-Fi hotspots, a map full of pushpins appears.

But Maps doesn't discern between free hotspots and ones you have to pay for. And Maps doesn't offer a review of the hotspot's signal quality. And although Maps is plenty easy to use, we know an ever better, easier way. It's called JiWire Wi-Fi Finder, which has a clean, easy-to-use interface that makes it easy to search for hotspots in more than 150,000 locations in 135 countries. It also allows you to limit your search to free hotspots, as shown in Figure 16-1.

After tapping the Go button, a list of hotspot locations appears. Tap the name of a found hotspot, and you see another screen with its name, address, phone number, and three buttons: Call, Map, and Info. The Call and Map buttons do what you'd expect: dial the phone number and display the location in the Maps

Figure 16-1: JiWire Wi-Fi Finder is a better way to find Wi-Fi hotspots.

application, respectively. But the Info button is the best; it tells you more about the business and the quality of its wireless network, as shown in Figure 16-2.

It's easy to use, it's elegant, it does stuff Maps doesn't, and best of all, it's free. How can you not love that? Go to `http://iphone.jiwire.com`.

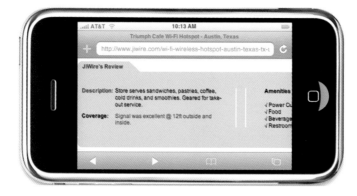

Figure 16-2: Most hotspots have mini-reviews.

A Double-Threat for Everything iPhone

If you're looking for a Web site that offers a little bit of almost everything an iPhone user might want, look no further than iPhoneAppr. If you visit the site on a Mac or a PC, you'll see a full-scale Web site with news, chat forums, applications, tutorials, and a blog, as shown in Figure 16-3.

But if you use your iPhone to visit the site, you get a streamlined interface designed for the device that focuses on the latest and greatest applications (that is, Web sites), as shown in Figure 16-4.

Figure 16-3: The Web browser look of iPhoneAppr.

iPhoneAppr is updated several times a day and always seems to have the scoop on the latest and newest sites for the iPhone. Several other sites have lists of iPhone applications, but iPhoneAppr is slicker, easier to use on both the computer and the iPhone, and usually more timely than the others.

To get there from your computer, go to `http://www.iphoneappr.com`. From your iPhone, go to `http://www.iphoneappr.com/iphone`.

Fast, Easy Shopping with OneTrip Shopping List

No matter how good an iPhone typist you are, we have a faster, easier way to make shopping lists. It's called OneTrip Shopping List. Rather than typing items for a list, you tap them. Here's how it works. First, tap a category. Then tap an item or items in the category, as shown in Figure 16-5.

Figure 16-4: The iPhone look of iPhoneAppr.

Figure 16-5: First tap a category (left), and then tap an item or items in that category (right).

At the store, you tap the items as you toss them into your shopping cart, and a check mark magically appears next to their name, as shown in Figure 16-6.

You can edit a list any time you like, and you can type any item not included in one of the categories. And with another tap you can e-mail the list to yourself or anyone you want.

OneTrip Shopping List has one last great feature — it's free. Go to `http://onetrip.org/onetrip/`.

Figure 16-6: A OneTrip Shopping List shopping list.

Calculating Tips Has Never Been Easier

Sure you can use the iPhone's calculator to figure out how much of a tip to leave, but using Danny Goodman's Tip Calculator, at `http://dannyg.com/iphone/tipCalc`, is a whole lot easier. Just tap the Food & Bevs or Tax field and a numeric keypad pops up on the screen, as shown in Figure 16-7.

After you specify the number of diners and the amounts for food and tax, the Tip Calculator does the rest, calculating the gratuity, total, and total amount per diner, as shown in Figure 16-8.

Figure 16-7: A handy numeric keypad for calculating tips.

Figure 16-8: Specify the number of diners and the amount of food, drink, and tax; the Tip Calculator does the rest.

If you tap the little *i* to the left of Gratuity you can even choose how the tip is calculated — as a percent of the food and beverage total or as a multiple of the sales tax.

Tip Calculator, like the other items in this chapter, is 100% free of charge, leaving you extra cash to be a generous tipper.

Match Three Gems (Free)

Bejeweled, at www.popcap.com, is a free "match three gems" game you play on your iPhone. If you've ever played Bejeweled on the Mac or the PC, it's the same but designed for your iPhone.

For those unfamiliar with this enjoyable and addictive game, the goal is to arrange three or more matching gems in a line either horizontally or vertically. To move the gems, you tap one, and then tap any adjacent gem to swap their places, as shown in Figure 16-9.

A swap occurs only if it will form a line of three or more matching gems. In Figure 16-9, swapping the yellow and green gems creates a horizontal line of three green gems as shown in Figure 16-10. The three green gems will then disappear, the gems above them will slide downward to fill in the gaps, and new gems fall from the top of the board to fill in any gaps.

The more lines of three or more gems you make, the higher your score. The game ends when no more lines of three or more matching gems can be created.

Figure 16-9: I tapped the yellow gem first, and then the green gem on its left.

Figure 16-10: The horizontal line of three green gems will now disappear, the gems above the line of green gems will drop down to replace them, and new gems will appear to fill in the empty spaces.

Practice Typing

By now you've probably done a fair share of typing using the iPhone's multitouch keyboard. Some of you may still be struggling with it. For others, let's just say you're getting a tad cocky. "Look at me. I'm hot stuff. This keyboard thing is really a piece of cake."

Think so? Why not put your skills to the test? That's what the iPhone Typing Test site (http://www.iphonetypingtest.com/) is all about. You can try your hand, um, fingers at two types of tests.

In the first test, your goal is to type a sentence as quickly and accurately as possible. The sentence appears in a yellow box at the top of the screen. The test begins when you tap inside the blue field just below the yellow field. At that moment, the sentence you are trying to match and the virtual keyboard appear simultaneously, as Figure 16-11 shows.

When you are finished typing, tap Done to see how you fared, as shown in Figure 16-12. Are you still feeling cocky?

Figure 16-11: Try to match the sentence in the yellow field by typing in the blue field.

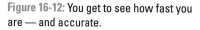

Figure 16-12: You get to see how fast you are — and accurate.

The second exam is a freestyle test in which you get to type anything you want for as long as you want. When you tap Done, your words-per-minute are calculated. Before leaving the site, check out the typing tips section.

An Instant Messaging Workaround

We were surprised that instant messaging was among the features Apple left out when the iPhone was launched. Apple has long included a fine IM program called iChat on Macs. And IM is a popular feature on some rival cell phones.

Apple may well add a version of iChat on the iPhone, possibly even by the time you read this. But if they haven't gotten around to it yet, check out JiveTalk from BeeJive (`http://iphone.beejive.com/`).

The site was still in an early alpha testing stage as this book was being prepared, but you could already head there and log onto your existing AOL Instant Messenger (AIM), Google Talk, ICQ, Jabber, MSN Messenger, and Yahoo Messenger accounts.

It's easy to set up these accounts so they'll work through JiveTalk. Tap the + button at the JiveTalk home screen, and then tap the downward arrow next to the Network field to choose an IM network from the list that appears at the bottom of the screen, as shown in Figure 16-13. Tap Done and enter your username and password. If you so choose, tap the Save Account checkbox so you don't have to enter this information every time you want to engage in an IM session.

You can log into all your IM accounts at the same time. Your compadres across all your accounts appear in one integrated buddy list (shown in Figure 16-14); the little icon next to a name indicates which IM account he or she is associated with.

Figure 16-13: Adding an IM network.

As Figure 16-15 shows, the virtual keyboard slides up from the bottom the moment you tap the text box to type a message to a buddy. Per usual, the keyboard offers suggestions if it thinks you mistyped a word (which, as we discovered in the preceding section, does indeed happen). The actual IM dialog appears in text bubbles.

Figure 16-14: All your buddies across different accounts turn up in one place.

Figure 16-15: What a text exchange looks like inside JiveTalk.

Through the JiveTalk's settings, you can choose whether or not to display offline buddies, show status messages, and display emoticons (smiley faces and the like).

Wassup with Widgets?

Lots of sites can help you find iPhone widgets, those "lite" but useful mini applications that range from a handy little version of the periodic table of the elements to a cheap gas finder.

One of the most comprehensive widget finders we've come across is the aptly named iPhone Widget List, at `http://iphonewidgetlist.com/`. Figure 16-16 shows what the site looks like.

Listed apps carry user ratings and status updates (the widget works, roughly working, proof of concept, beta, and so on). You can also tap a See it Now button to get a closer peek at the widget.

Figure 16-16: A master repository of widgets.

iPhone Network Speed Tester

Ever wonder if your Internet connection — Wi-Fi or EDGE — was faster or slower than average? If so, you're going to enjoy using the iPhone Network Test at http://www.iphonenetworktest.com/. Just tap the Start Test link on the front page, and after a few seconds your network speed appears, as shown in Figure 16-17.

Kbps (kilobits per second) are a common measure of your data transfer rate. A kilobit is 1000 bits, so one kilobit per second equals 1000 bits per second.

If you tap the link for EDGE or Wi-Fi below the words "How are you connected to the Internet," your EDGE or Wi-Fi speed is recorded for posterity. Then, if you tap the Results button that appears (and also appears on the front page of the site), you see the average speeds for all network tests, all Wi-Fi tests, and all EDGE tests, as shown in Figure 16-18.

Figure 16-17: The network speed for this test was 1541.5 kbps.

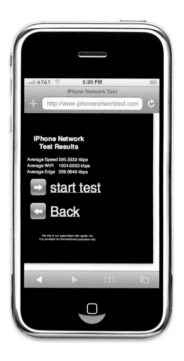

Figure 16-18: Tap the Results button for the average speed for all tests, all Wi-Fi tests, and all EDGE tests.

What can we discern from all this? Well, our Wi-Fi speed of 1541.5 kbps is around 1.5 times the average Wi-Fi test speed. Put another way, this Wi-Fi connection is pretty darn fast.

Read Your Fortune

"Your great attention to detail is both a blessing and a curse." "It takes more than good memory to have good memories." "There is a true and sincere friendship between you and your friends."

Profound thoughts, huh?

We picked up these pearls of wisdom at iPhone Fortune Cookie 1.0, at `http://m.digitaljoven.com/fortune/index.html`. When you first arrive at this amusing site, you see the fortune cookie shown at the top of Figure 16-19.

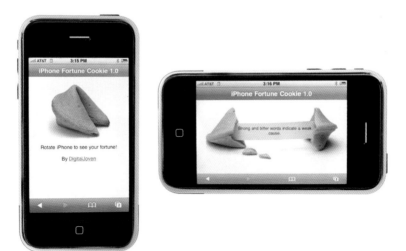

Figure 16-19: Your fortune is hidden inside this cookie until you rotate your iPhone sideways to break it in half.

Then when you rotate the phone to landscape mode, the cookie breaks in half and your fortune is revealed, as shown in the figure on the bottom. Repeat this little drill to request another fortune. Alas, some of the fortunes are as stale as the cookies we've eaten in real Chinese restaurants. Samples: "A pleasant surprise is in store for you." "You will live a long, happy life."

Guess that's just the way the cookie crumbles. (Hey, we couldn't help ourselves.)

Ten Helpful Hints, Tips, and Shortcuts

In This Chapter

▷ Faster typing with "the slide"

▷ Faster typing with autocorrection

▷ Viewing the iPhone's capacity

▷ Syncing notes

▷ Exploiting links

▷ Sharing Web pages

▷ Revving up Edge

▷ Faking a home page

▷ Storing stuff

▷ Dandy docking

After spending a lot of quality time with our iPhones, it's only natural that we've discovered more than a few helpful hints, tips, and shortcuts. In this chapter we share some of our faves.

Do the Slide for Accuracy and Punctuation

Here's a tip that will help you type faster in two ways. First, it will help you type more accurately; second, it will let you type punctuation and numerals faster than ever before.

Over the course of this book you've found out how to tap, how to double-tap, and even how to double-tap with two fingers. Now we want to introduce you to a new gesture we like to call "the slide."

To do the slide, you start by performing the first half of a tap. That is, you touch your finger to the screen but don't lift it up. Now, without lifting your finger, slide it onto the key you want to type. You'll know you're on the right key because it will pop up (enlarge).

First try it during normal typing. Stab at a key and if you miss, rather than lifting off, backspacing, and trying again, do the slide onto the proper key. Once you get the hang of it, you'll see that it saves a lot of time and improves your accuracy as well.

Now here's the best part: You can use the slide to save time with punctuation and numerals, too. The next time you need to type a punctuation mark or number, try this technique:

1. **Start a slide action with your finger on the .?123 key (the key to the left of the Space key when the alphabetical keyboard is active).**

   This is a slide, not a tap, so don't lift your finger just yet.

2. **When the punctuation and numeric keyboard appears on the screen, slide your finger onto the punctuation mark or number you want to type.**

3. **Lift your finger.**

The cool thing is that the punctuation and numeric keyboard disappears and the alphabetical keyboard reappears all without tapping the .?123 key to display the punctuation and numeric keyboard, and without tapping the *ABC* key (the key to the left of the Space key when the punctuation and numeric keyboard is active).

Practice these two techniques and we guarantee that in a few days you'll be typing faster and more accurately.

Don't Bother with Don't

While on the subject of punctuation, you can type *dont* to get to *don't*, and *cant* to get to *can't*. We've told you to put some faith in the iPhone's auto-correction software. And that applies to contractions. In other words, let the iPhone's intelligent keyboard insert the apostrophes on your behalf for these and other common words and save time.

We're aware of at least one exception. The iPhone cannot distinguish between *it's* the contraction of "it is" and *its* the possessive adjective and possessive pronoun.

Here you thought you were buying a tech book and you get a grammar lesson thrown in at no extra charge. Just think of us as full service authors.

Three Ways to View the iPhone's Capacity

When your iPhone is selected in the source list in iTunes, you see a colorful chart at the bottom of the screen that tells you how your iPhone's capacity is being used by your media and other data.

By default, the chart shows the amount of space your audio, video, and photo files use on your iPhone in GB or MB. But you knew that. What you probably don't know is that when you click the colorful chart, it cycles through two slightly different displays. The first click changes the display from space used to the number of items. The second click changes the display to the total playing time (Audio and Video only), as shown in Figure 17-1.

This is particularly helpful before you go on a trip. Knowing that you have 5.5 hours of video and 1.8 days of audio is far more useful than knowing how many gigabytes you're packing.

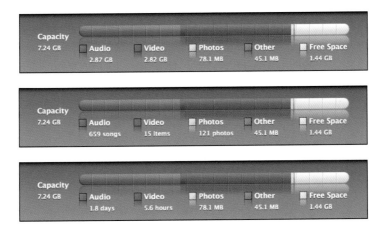

Figure 17-1: Click the colorful chart, and what's stored on your iPhone is expressed in different ways.

Assault on batteries

Because this is a chapter of tips and hints, and we consider it important to help you not run out of juice before you're ready, we'd be remiss if we didn't include some ways you can extend your battery life (even if it does cause this "Part of Tens" chapter to contain more than ten items).

First and foremost: If you use a carrying case for your iPhone, charging the phone while it's in that case may generate more heat than is healthy for your phone. Overheating is bad for both battery capacity and battery life, so if your iPhone gets a little toasty when you charge it in its case, take it out of the case before you charge it.

Bluetooth consumes power even when it's not being used. If you're not using a Bluetooth device (such as a headset or car kit), make sure Bluetooth is turned off. To do so, tap Settings on the Home screen, tap General, tap Bluetooth, and then tap the On/Off switch if necessary to turn off Bluetooth.

Just as Bluetooth consumes power even when you're not using it, so does Wi-Fi, so turn it off when you're not using it. Tap Settings on the Home screen, then tap General, Network, Wi-Fi, and then tap the On/Off switch if necessary to turn off Wi-Fi.

Activating Auto-Brightness allows the screen brightness to adjust based on current lighting conditions. This can be easier on your battery than cranking it up and leaving it set to a bright setting. To activate this feature, tap Settings on the Home screen, tap Brightness, and then tap its On/Off switch if necessary to turn it on.

Finally, turning on EQ (equalizer; see Chapter 7 for details) when you listen to music can make it sound better, but it also uses more processing power. Turning off EQ will help your battery last longer. If you've added EQ to tracks in iTunes via the Track Info window and you want to retain the EQ from iTunes, set the EQ on your iPhone to flat. Since you're not turning off EQ, your battery life will be slightly worse. But your songs will sound just the way you expect them to sound. Either way, to alter your EQ settings, tap Settings on the Home screen, tap iPod, and then tap EQ.

According to Apple, a properly maintained iPhone battery will retain up to 80% of its original capacity after 400 full charge and discharge cycles. But you can replace the battery at any time if it no longer holds sufficient charge to meet your needs.

Your one-year limited warranty includes the replacement of a defective battery. If you choose to extend your coverage to two years with the AppleCare Protection Plan for the iPhone, Apple will replace the battery if it drops below 50% of its original capacity.

If your iPhone is out of warranty, Apple will replace the battery for $79.00, plus $6.95 shipping, plus local tax, and then dispose of your old battery in an environmentally friendly manner.

So You Want to Sync Notes, Do You?

As you've no doubt discovered by now, there's no easy way to synchronize notes between iPhone's Notes application and your computer.

If you'd like to sync a note or notes, though, we know of a kludge. Rather than using the Notes application, you use your contact manager program and the Contacts list in the Phone application. Each contact has its own notes field and each notes field can contain a pretty good amount of text.

So the kludge is to create fake contacts and use their notes fields for notes you want to sync. Then, after you sync, and assuming you remember the name(s) of your fake contact(s), the notes will appear on both your phone and your computer.

It may not be the most elegant solution, but it does work.

Tricks with Links and Phone Numbers

The iPhone does something special when it encounters phone numbers or URLs in e-mail and SMS text messages. For example, the iPhone interprets as a phone number any sequence of numbers that looks like a phone number — #-###-###-####, ###-####, #.###.###.#### and so on. The same goes for sequences of characters that look like a Web address (URL), such as `http://www.WebSite Name.com` or `www.WebSiteName.com`. When that happens they appear as blue links on your screen. Tap them and the iPhone does the right thing. It launches the Phone application and dials the number for phone numbers, or launches Safari and takes you to the appropriate Web page for URLs.

That's useful but somewhat expected. What's more useful and not so expected is the way Safari handles phone numbers and URLs.

Let's start with phone numbers. When you encounter a phone number on a Web page, give it a tap. A little dialog box appears on the screen displaying that phone number and offering you a choice of two buttons: Call or Cancel. Tap Call to switch to the Phone application and dial the number; tap Cancel to return to the Web page.

Here's another cool Safari trick, this time with links. If you press and hold on a link rather than tapping it, a little floating text bubble appears and shows you the underlying URL.

The same thing happens if you press and hold on a URL in Mail or Text, which we find even more useful because it enables you to spot bogus links without switching to Safari or actually visiting the URL.

Share the Love

Ever stumble upon a Web page you just have to share with a buddy? The iPhone makes its dead simple. From the site in question, tap the address field at the top of the browser. Then tap the Share button that appears in the upper-left corner of the screen. Upon doing so, the Mail program opens. The subject line is already pre-populated with the name of the Web site you're visiting. And the URL appears in the area in which you can compose a message. Type whatever you want to say and supply your pal's e-mail address. Send it along like any e-mail.

Make Web Browsing with EDGE Up to Five Times Faster!

When we saw this tip on the Web (at www.iPhonePOV.com), we tried it immediately and were thrilled to discover that it really does make Web surfing over AT&T's EDGE data network much faster.

While having the "real" Internet on your iPhone is a blessing, the preponderance of pages with complex JavaScripts and annoying blinking ads can make using EDGE to access those pages a curse. Unfortunately, EDGE just doesn't have the bandwidth for such frippery.

So here's the workaround: The trick is to access the Web via a proxy server that strips all the stuff you don't need, such as blinking ads, pop-ups, and other flashy but useless components, leaving only the good content for you to enjoy. More or less.

Fortunately, one of iPhonePOV's graphic designers has a cousin who knows someone who works at Google, and they convinced her to have Google set up a proxy server for the iPhone and keep it a secret from every Web site except iPhonePOV.com.

We'd like to pause here for a moment to thank both iPhonePOV and Google. You ROCK!

To surf the Web up to five times faster, follow these instructions to access the Google Mobile proxy server on your iPhone:

1. **Tap the Safari icon on your Home screen.**

2. **Enter the URL: http://www.google.com/m.**

   The m stands for mobile.

3. **Scroll down to the bottom of the page and tap Mobile under the words "View Google in."**

   If you can't tap Mobile because it's not a link, you're already viewing Google in its Mobile mode.

4. **Tap the link for Settings a couple of lines above "View Google in."**

5. **Find the Format Pages for Your Mobile Phone setting and tap the button to turn it on.**

6. **Scroll down and tap the Save button at the bottom of the page.**

The Google Mobile page reappears and from this point forward, anything you search for or link to from Google Mobile is formatted for faster loading by

Google's Mobile proxy server. Use the Search box on the Google Mobile page and every site on the Web is diddled to appear quickly on your iPhone.

If you visit a page through the proxy server and know you want to revisit it someday, bookmark it. Tap that bookmark and the faster-loading Google Mobile version of the page loads.

The only downside is that every so often you actually want to see the frippery that the Google Mobile proxy server strips off a page. No problem. Just scroll to the bottom of the Google Mobile page, look for "View Google in," and tap the link to Classic. The "real" version of Google loads and you can search for and visit pages the old, slower way.

If you are interested in the back-story on why this works (which has to do with older mobile phones and something called WAP), we suggest you read the original tip at: http://www.iphonepov.com/2007/06/iphone-browsing-with-edge-5x-faster.html.

Once again, thanks to iPhonePOV and Google for taking some of the sting out of using EDGE.

Choosing a Home Page for Safari

You may have noticed that there's no home page Web site on the iPhone version of Safari as there is in the Mac and PC version of the browser (and for that matter every other Web browser we know of). Instead, when you tap the Safari icon, you return to the last site you visited.

The folks at *Macworld* have a suggested workaround. Just create a bookmark for your favorite site and drag it to the top of the bookmarks list (following the instructions in Chapter 10). It's not a perfect remedy, but it will get you home that much faster.

Storing Files

A tiny Massachusetts software company known as Ecamm Network is selling an inexpensive piece of Mac OS X software that lets you copy files from your computer to your iPhone and copy files from the iPhone to a computer. (There is no Windows version.) Better still, you can try the $9.95 program called iPhoneDrive for a week before deciding whether you want to buy it. Go to www.ecamm.com to fetch the free demo.

In a nutshell, here's how it works. After downloading the software onto your Mac, double-click the program's icon to start it. You'll see the window displayed in Figure 17-2.

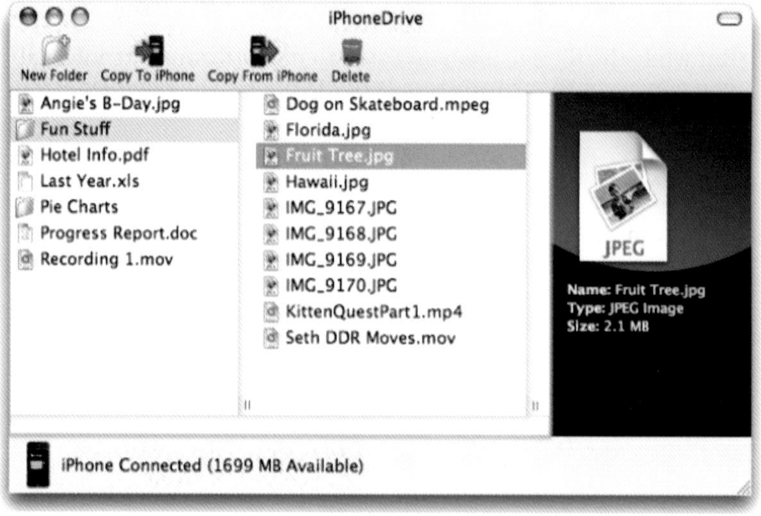

Figure 17-2: The iPhoneDrive file browser and toolbar.

To transfer files and folders to the iPhone (assuming there's room on the device), click the Copy to iPhone button on the toolbar and click to select the files you want to copy. The files are copied into the appropriate folder on the iPhone. Alternatively, drag files and folders from the Mac desktop or a Finder window into the iPhoneDrive browser.

To go the other way and copy files from your iPhone to your computer, highlight the files or folders you want copied, and click the Copy from iPhone button on the toolbar. Select the destination on your Mac where you want to store the files and then click Save.

You can also drag files or folders from the iPhoneDrive browser into a Finder window or the desktop. Or double-click a file to download it to the Mac's Documents folder.

But there are limitations. iPhoneDrive doesn't provide access to music synced in iTunes or photos taken with iPhone's camera. What's more, iPhoneDrive is for storage only, so you can't access any data on the iPhone's screen.

Stupid Dock Tricks

Ostensibly the purpose of the iPhone dock is to synch the device with your computer and, oh yeah, charge the device while doing so (provided your computer hasn't fallen asleep or isn't in standby mode).

But while the iPhone lets you listen to music through its internal speakers, you may want to take advantage of the dock's line out connector on the back to hook up superior powered speakers.

By the way, we ran across one posting at www.iphonetipoftheday.com suggesting that plugging the iPhone into its cradle acts as a mini-subwoofer to amplify music played back through the iPhone 's own speakers. Frankly, we had a hard time hearing any difference.

Apple itself maintains that speakerphone calls sound better when the iPhone is docked because of something called audio porting.

Separate from all that, we discovered one other unintended if imperfect benefit of a docked iPhone; you can snap a picture without the camera shaking.

Index

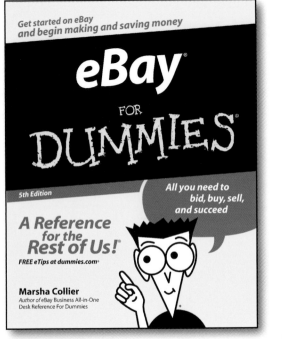

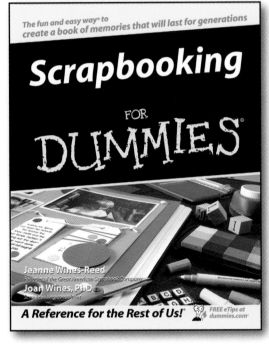